MW00606396

# A Wise Woman Builds Her House

Huldah Dauid

The Awakening Remnant Koalition
California

Copyright © 2017 by Maureka Davis

All rights reserved. No part of this publication may be reproduced, distributed or transmitted in any form or by any means, including photocopying, recording, or other electronic or mechanical methods, without the prior written permission of the publisher, except in the case of brief quotations embodied in critical reviews and certain other noncommercial uses permitted by copyright law. For permission requests, write to the publisher, addressed "Attention: Permissions Coordinator," at the address below.

Huldah Dauid/The Awakening Remnant
HuldahDauid@HerRoyalRoots.com
www.HerRoyalRoots.com

Book Layout ©2013 BookDesignTemplates.com

Ordering Information:
Quantity sales. Special discounts are available on quantity purchases by corporations, associations, and others. For details, contact the "Special Sales Department" at the email address above.
A Wise Woman Builds Her House/ Huldah Dauid. —1st ed.
ISBN-10: 0-9986926-1-1
ISBN-13: 978-0-9986926-1-6

# Contents

i

*This book is dedicated to every woman, who at one time or another, expressed the willingness to build her "house", but lacked the necessary tools to do so.*

# INTRODUCTION

*Seek ye Yahuah while he may be found, call ye upon him while he is near: Let the wicked forsake his way, and the unrighteous man his thoughts: and let him return unto Yahuah, and he will have mercy upon him; and to our Elohim, for he will abundantly pardon. For my thoughts are not your thoughts, neither are your ways my ways, saith Yahuah. For as the heavens are higher than the earth, so are my ways higher than your ways, and my thoughts than your thoughts.*

**Isaiah 55:6-9**

## Why just definitions?

If you know anything about me (Huldah), you know that the will of the Father often baffles me. Trying to navigate through what I believe I need and what the Father has placed on my heart was a hard battle with this particular work. The original intent of this book was to create a series of lessons that each woman could study like a devotional, but once I began, the Father wanted me to do something different. He wanted me to give the tools and for the reader/studier to dig deeper into His word. As much as I enjoy being a companion on your journey of discovery, my partnership will be limited this time. By limited, I mean that I am only transferring the words. It will be your job to study these word meanings in the Word and apply them to your life.

## Building a House

The book is titled <u>A Wise Woman Builds Her House</u> because the function of a "house" is critical in having a Scripturally sound home, and the way that it is constructed is pivotal to its sustainability. Each house contains similar building blocks. For example, each house needs a door for an entrance, each house needs a window for light to illuminate within, each house needs a foundation that is able to endure troubled times and whether it can withstand, each house needs strong walls for protection from the elements and dangers without. These are the sheer basics.

Likewise, some things are not a necessity but add character to the home, such as, where you place your window if you choose a tall door or a red door—it's a matter of choice. The same is similar to the nature of this book and with how you choose to tackle the word studies. The Hebrew meaning and the Scriptural context are given. This information will aid in your ability to interpret without violating the text with how you "feel." In Torah, feelings are not applied to commandments and cannot be used to change or negate any part of the Word as it has been delivered from Yahuah.

## Why Should I use <u>A Wise Woman Builds Her House</u> instead of lexicon or a Biblical dictionary?

The question is going to come up: Why shouldn't I just use a lexicon or dictionary to look up these words? The simple answer would be: How is that working out for us? But the more serious answer is, we have lots of tools and dictionaries that have served a purpose, but they are lacking when it comes to defining words Hebraically for Hebrews. Because each person is in a different place on their walk and understanding of the

Hebrew language, I included the Strong's number next each definition. The numbers are used because there will be times where words are defined, and a person will want to know why these words do not line up with what my dictionary says.

Through study, you will find that often the word that is used in English to define a word could be utilized for several different Hebrew words. For instance, the word for 'law' in Hebrew is Torah; but there are also other words that mean 'teaching 'that is also translated as law, leading the reader to believe that each time it says 'law' we should not do those things (not knowing that all 'law' is 'teaching' and all teachings of Scripture are Torah). In a basic word look-up, it will only render the word that directly defines that word in the verse; and not understand all the other words in Hebrew that have the same meaning but different function based on context. (E.g. Study 24: chastising) In this study, you will not only learn that chastising is important, but also how every punishment is carried out the same way. Reading is Fundamental

In each study, you will find the most common Hebrew word for the English translation. The Hebrew word is written in both modern script and pictorial script. The pictorial Hebrew is a tool to aid you in understanding why a Hebrew would have chosen the definition. Remember that Hebraically things are defined based on the elements that are around them (in an Eastern setting). This is why it is pivotal to refrain from defining words based upon where we are in captivity. Our location in the Diaspora (unless you are in the land, and even then, there are perversions that warrant caution) severely limits our ability to interpret the Word based purely on observation because we are in the land of confusion (Babylon), no matter where you are. In knowing this, it is important that you do not rely solely on the one verse that is given to define the word, but that you use a source to look up similar verses that also help to give you additional verses that mean the same thing and see how they are functioning in their different contextual understandings. A great online tool for this is BibleHub.com or if you like a book, Treasury of Scriptural Knowledge. These sources will provide you with all the verses that use the same Hebrew word (conjugation may be different) and how they are translated into English.

***Disclaimer: If you have not read the book in Scripture that a verse is being quoted from, STOP your study and read the book. Context in Scriptural study is in knowing the WHOLE book. Also, if you have not read TORAH (the first 5 books), STOP! Before you start this study, you need to know that all words and how they will be defined throughout the rest of Scripture have their root in Torah. This is called The Law of First Mention. You will see this when I have a word that is completely different use the same verse in the book of Genesis (or elsewhere in Torah) to define the same verse. If you do not know how the word was used, then you cannot begin to understand how to apply it.

Ariel, in Little Mermaid, is an awesome example of what it looks like to not know the function and to run with it. She was just making up words for objects never knowing how they functioned and what to do with them. In one scene in particular, she sits down with the prince and combs her hair with a fork. That is what it will look like if you have not read Torah and try to understand how these words function just from one verse. I know that was a simply a movie example, but I think it just helped what I said live for someone.

Why is each verse given in Hebrew and English?

First, so you know that I am not making any of this up; second, for you to see where the words are and begin to see them in the text. You will be surprised how much this will help you in learning the language and building your vocabulary. On an even simpler level, this will help you begin to spot the AlephBet if you are just trying to learn what those letters look like in the verses. Finally, you will begin to see the poetry and repetition of words for emphasis that you do not see in English. I encourage you to highlight and write notes in the margins when this happens.

## The Importance of Words

These words will help to connect them to stories in Scripture that will give you a much greater insight into how Yah wants (and does not want) your house to look. Every word in this book will teach both the negatives and positives attached to their implementation and will show the consequences of dysfunction we experience when we fail to properly apply the words to our lives. So, what is remarkable about words? Scripture teaches that Yah's Word sustains everything in the Universe and it is this Word that drives the actions and becomes the motivating factor for all we do.

*And He is before all things, and by Him all things consist.*

Colossians 1:17

*In the beginning was the Word, and the Word was with YAH, and the Word was YAH. He was with YAH in the beginning. Through Him all things were made, and without Him nothing was made that has been made.*

John 1:1-3

*He sendeth forth His commandment upon earth: His Word runneth very swiftly.*

Psalm 147:15

*By faith we understand that the universe was formed by YAH's command, so that what is seen was not made out of what was visible.*

Hebrews 11:3

*By the word of Yahuah were the heavens made; and all the host of them by the breath of his mouth.*

Psalm 33:6

When these words are ill-defined or even slightly changed the action and function of those elements (including humans) carrying out the command of the Words are also changed. Imagine getting a blueprint to build a house but every time you try to follow the instruction you find that the definition of the words is different than what you thought they meant. The frustration and the inability to complete the task are inevitable. The same has happened to everyone who has sought to follow the instructions of the words given in organized religion for relationships, spiritual growth, and childrearing. When you aim to do the will of the Word (blueprint), but the definitions change from translation to translation and from teacher to teacher, the frustration keeps you from effectively completing the task. What I have been led to do in this work is to relieve the frustration. The foundational materials are here before you. The nails are pre-packed; the wood is pre-cut, the foundation laid, and the necessary materials delivered to your fingertips. Your job is to follow the directions of the Ruach for how these elements should look in your life and where they need reinforcement.

As you go through each lesson, you will notice that there are New Testament verses that are used either at the beginning or end of the lessons. These verses are there to show you two things; the first is that all words in Scripture must be viewed through a Hebrew lens, and the second is to show you that all words in the Greek can be traced back to an original Hebrew root that will help you better understand how to carry out the ordinances that are restated in the New Testament. By making these terms more concrete, you can transform your mind into the mind of Christ (a Hebraic mind), allowing yourself to think closer to the will of the Father and keep you from praying and operating amiss, which is easily done when the Word of Yah is viewed and carried out through a Western lens.

## What is the "Western Lens"?

The Western lens is a viewpoint that operates in form (what something looks like) versus function (what something acts like). The Hebrew language and people are action based. Everything boils down to what something does and not what it looked like when it was doing it. Obedience to the Father and his Word should be the same way. As Hebraic women living in a Western-driven world, we have to stop viewing our function through the lens of the lands of our dispersion and start viewing our actions through the lens of our timeless and unchanging Father. Hebraic women in the Western world are caught on what it looks like to be a Hebrew and not so much on what the function of being a Hebrew is. Our lack of national transformation is based on the fact that we want it to look "right" and we have not yet fully come to grasp with what is right outside of how it is interpreted to us from men who are just as Western as we are. My hope is that as you begin to study these words they will give you the direction toward Hebraic functionality. If it functions, it is Hebrew. If I is dysfunctional, we must reevaluate.

Last, this is not a tool that you will go through once and have it. Every word and definition will not make sense on the surface. There are words and definitions here that continue to renew themselves every time I approach them. They gain new meanings, and they transform and stretch me more and more. I am praying that the same happens to you. The reality of the Word is that it does not work for you unless you work for it. Meaning, if you are not working to do what the Word says, then the Word will be stagnant; but as you begin to be obedient to Word, you will begin to create the blessing and transformation that all of us are seeking in our homes.

*Below you will find a key for the format of the definitions and transliterations.*

Transliterated Root

Pictographic Script

מעה (M-AhH) Strong's #4577, 4578/ AHLB #1292 The numbers are where they can be located in each source

A hidden thing that only Yah knows

An unknown that is known by a higher consciousness

Gut or lower region

Seat of Consciousness

Internal organs of the lower torso

AHLB (Ancient Hebrew Lexicon of the Bible)

Strongs (Strongs Concordance)

*And, behold, the word of Yahuah came unto him, saying, this shall not be thine heir; but he that shall come forth out of thine own **bowels** shall be thine heir.*

וְהִנֵּה דְבַר־יְהוָה אֵלָיו לֵאמֹר לֹא יִירָשְׁךָ זֶה כִּי־אִם אֲשֶׁר יֵצֵא **מִמֵּעֶיךָ** הוּא יִירָשֶׁךָ

Genesis 15:4

| Hebrew Definition | Modern Script | | Early Script | Picotoral Meaning | Sound | Numerical Value |
|---|---|---|---|---|---|---|
| STRONG, POWER, LEADER, SOURCE, | א | Aleph | | OX HEAD | SILENT LETTER | 1 |
| HOUSE, IN, FAMILY, WOMB | ב | Bet/Vet | | NOMADIC TENT FLOORPLAN | B as in Boy<br>V as in Vine | 2 |
| GO, TRAVEL, WALK, GATHER, CAMEL, CARRY, PERSUE | ג | Gimmel | | FOOT | G as in Girl | 3 |
| ENTRANCE, DOOR, PATH-WAY, DEMENSION, HANG | ד | Dalet | | TENT DOOR | D as in Door | 4 |
| WINDOW, THE, LOOK, REVEAL, BREATH, SIGH | ה | Hey | | MAN WITH RAISED HANDS | H as in Hat | 5 |
| ADD, SECURE, HOOK, NAIL, CONNECTION, AND | ו | Vav/Waw/Uau | | TENT PEG | V as in Vine<br>Ow as in WOW | 6 |
| PLOW, WEAPON, SWORD, DIG, CUT, THE WORD | ז | Zayin | | PLOUGH | Z as in Zebra | 7 |
| GROUP, FENCE, OUTSIDE, DIVIDE, SEPARATION, TENT WALL | ח | Chet | | TENT WALL | (Soft)<br>CH as in baCH | 8 |
| SURROUND, CONTAIN, MUD, SERPENT | ט | Tet | | BASKET | T as in Toy | 9 |
| ARM, HAND, REACH, WORK, THROW, WORSHIP, DEED | י | Yod | | HAND AND ARM | Y as in Yard | 10 |
| BEND, OPEN, ALLOW, TAME, CUP, BLESSING, PALM, RECEIVE | כ | Kaph | | OPEN PALM | K as in Kite<br>CH as in BaCH | 20 |
| TEACH, INSTRUCT, YOKE, BIND, MOVE, TOWARD, FORCE | ל | Lamed | | SHEPHERD STAFF/ GOAD | L as in Light | 30 |
| MOTION, CHAOS, MIGHTY, BLOOD | מ | Mem | | WATER | M as in Moon | 40 |
| CONTINUE, HEIR, SON, MANIFEST, SPERM | נ | Nun | | SPROUTING SEED | N as in Night | 50 |
| HOLD, PROTECT, PROP, SUPPORT | ס | Samech | | THORN | S as in Sun | 60 |
| SEE, VISION, PROTECTION, FORCUS, WATCH, EXPERIENCE | ע | Ayin | | EYE | SILENT LETTER | 70 |
| TALK, BLOW, SCATTER, SPEAK | פ | Peh/Feh | | MOUTH | P as in Put<br>F as in Far | 80 |
| WAIT, CHASE, SNARE, HUNT, FISH, | צ | Tsade | | MAN ON HIS SIDE | Ts as in nuTs | 90 |
| CONDENSE, CIRCLE, TIME | ק | Qoph | | SUN AT THE HORIZON | Q as in Queen | 100 |
| FIRST, BEGINNING, TOP, HEAD, HIGH, CHEIF | ר | Resh | | HEAD OF A MAN | R as in Rake | 200 |
| SHARP, PRESS, EAT, CONSUME, DESTROY, FIRE, TWO DANGLERS (BREAST) | ש | Shin/Sin | | TWO FRONT TEETH | Sh as in Shore<br>S as in Sand | 300 |
| MARK, SIGN, SIGNATURE, CROSS | ת | Tav/Taw/Tau | | TWO CROSSED STICKS | T as in Tall | 400 |

## ~Read Before You Begin~

I have completed the first two studies for you. These lessons serve as an example of what you can accomplish with each set of words and how you will be able to uncover deeper meaning within familiar texts and verses. Please remember that your journey to building your house will be different but the blueprint and the definition of the words do not change. We cannot add to or take away from the Word (Deut. 4:2), so when in doubt about the application of a word set be sure err on the side of needing to dive deeper. Be sure to use the Hebrew chart as a guide during your study. Also, never settle for something that cannot be supported by Torah and that you have taken out of context. I pray that in this journey you can use the Word of Yah to unlock His will and function for your house. Don't forget to be patient and to use understanding as you approach each set of words and allow the Ruach to move.

Shalom,

# Peace: Shalom (שלום)

# ᴀᴀᴠᴜᴌᴌ

*For I know the thoughts that I think toward you, saith
Yahuah, thoughts of peace, and not of evil, to give you an expected end.*
**Jeremiah 29:11**

People who often define peace do so through a very narrow and often personally bias lens that is connected internal wishes for a moment of isolation to gather thoughts and/or to rest from the hustle and bustle of daily life. These individual thoughts and experiences often drive how we define and react to *peace*, which in turn motivates how we pursue it. Peace is more than what can be seen on the surface. Peace is likened the image of a swan resting peacefully on a calm glassy lake. The image is often admired and coveted for its serene effects, but what goes unnoticed is the most impactful. Though the swan seems to be inactive she is doing something beneath the water that ensures the tranquil scene that everyone loves, she is paddling her feet and moving in a manner that ensure her position of stillness on the water. Her peace

1

requires action. Often, when a translator attempts to bring the thought and function to any language something can be lost or poorly conveyed due to the culture and the understating in which it was originally written not properly translating over. Simply put, it can be difficult. Like the swan there is the initial understanding of what peace is from the vantage point of the onlooker but there is a completely different idea of peace when view it from the position of the swan. If we fail to do this then we can miss what the Highest is trying to show us when it comes to achieving and working toward peace. Fortunately, in this case of translation the English does not leave us far off base from the concrete understanding of the Hebrew. In English, 'peace' is freedom from disturbance, tranquility, cessation of war, or to remain silent. This is a decent definition of peace; however, it is only a partial report. 'Peace' in its current English form does not give any idea of how (like the swan's feet) to achieve peace other than stopping or ceasing an activity or function (similar to merely viewing the outcome of the swan on the water). Yes, there is an intellectual understanding of peace, but as we explore further we should be able to see how to re-store, live, and understand peace in every situation.

In Hebrew, the word for 'peace' is seen in two different root words. These two words offer different perspectives to the word 'peace' although they both connect to the same goal. The first is the root *Shlm* and the second is the word *Damah/Damm*. The root for *Shalom* is spelled שלם, and its pictorial spelling is ᴍᴜᴌᴌᴌ. The other word is *Damah* (and *Damm*), spelled ( דמה דמם,), and the pictorial spelling is ᴍᴀᴍᴛ (Please refer to the Hebrew chart in the appendix for the pictorial meanings).

*Damm* is the Hebrew word for blood. The literal translation means to refrain from speech, action, quieting, and repression. The reason these words are used to define blood in an action form is because when a person or animal sheds blood, he/she/it is then silenced. The three-letter root *dalet / mem / hey* means 'to move in a balanced way.' This word symbolizes the same connotation and relation to blood. Blood moves in a balanced way in the Universe. When blood is shed or when life is silenced, it is then given back to the ground; and there must either be restitution paid for the life or it is a cycle which been completed and causes the body to naturally return to the ground producing peace, rest, and balance. This is the circle of life.

The second root word is the most familiar form of peace. This Hebrew word for peace is *Shalom*. The root of the word is *shin / lamed / final mem.* שלם is defined as being complete or whole. In the Hebraic sense, achieving a positive outcome does not only happen by experiencing positivity. שלם can exist by adding or subtracting possessions, people, health, or comforts for the sake of restitution or recompense. שלם can also mean 'to draw out.' When Yah decides to draw out, it is always to restore something back to its proper position or place. The Father often draws out or quiets one's surroundings to minister to the heart of an individual for an intended purpose. Yah separates those who are dear to Him to repair or restore the inner self. The restoration of the inner self *is* the restoration back to Torah. This is seen respectively in the lives of the children of Israel in their removal from the land which he had given them land to restore peace between them, the land, and their El. Yah allows captivity to draw out Israel's sins through chastisement and affliction. This teaches them that there is no better place than within His care. He removed them from the land because they have polluted it with the magnitude of their sins and transgression, so the land cries out to also be restored. Last, the Covenant must be renewed and restored. This process is the cyclical process of restitution. It starts and ends with Yahuah. Inner self, place, position, as well as Covenant, are all renewed in the process of shalom. Yahuah desires for each person to achieve *Shalom* in their homes and their inner selves so they can operate as a vessel of righteousness for His glory. Just as a parent uses different tactics to draw out the best in their children, Yahuah uses the process of silence, removal, and then restoration to bring *Shalom* to His Chosen people.

## Application

In the opening Scripture, the Highest is speaking to the prophet Jeremiah regarding His Chosen people who are about to enter into Babylonian captivity. He is giving instructions on what to do while they are in captivity and how to ensure a return from captivity. One may ask, "Why not just keep them out of captivity all together and avoid the grueling monologue?" but that is not how the Father operates. A good father understands that the pursuit of restoration, where peace and tranquility exist, is not always done by keeping silent, avoiding war, or allowing freedom, but sometimes peace comes in obscure, hard-to-grasp-to-the-Western-mind ways. Although the children of Israel are being carried captive into a nation, Yah is commanding that they seek peace where they go and pray unto Yahuah "for peace and in that peace will they have peace" (Jeremiah 29:7). Yahuah goes on to warn them that others will try and convince them of strange doctrines and teachings through prophecy and divination, so they should ignore them, because they are not sent from Him and are liars. Yahuah gives reassurance by stating that after 70 years is accomplished, He will visit the children of Israel and perform His good word toward them and cause them to return to this place (Jeremiah 29:8-10). This verse confirms the process and the cyclical nature of Scripture: peace with the Creator, harmony with one another, and restoration to the promised land as the ultimate goal. Now how we as finite creatures would go about that process and how the infinite Creator brings peace about is a what we must learn and truly embrace.

Yah's view of peace and man's view of peace is completely different. To better understand peace and Yahuah's right-ruling in all circumstances, a person must first remove the mind of a tyrant god and replace it with the image of a loving parent (Father). Knowing that a person first loves you completely changes the way we receive their chastening.

*He who withholds his rod hates his child, but he who loves him gives him discipline.*
**Proverbs 13:24**

You will study the Hebrew word chastisement in a later study, but in this current context, it is much better to be disciplined in love than in hate. Many people have a problem with Yahuah and His "blind eye" towards His children during the dangerous and harmful situations over the course of their Diaspora. The sentiment is typically vocalized as "Where was God during slavery?" or "Where was God when these curses were overtaking us?" It is hard to fathom that the Father saw the atrocities which befell on His people as they endured these curses and did nothing. Could a good father sit in his high and lofty seat and watch as children are killed, women are raped, and men are beaten beyond recognition in the name of "God?" How can *that* be love, and how can prosperity flourish in such dysfunction?

Before one jumps to conclusions, a simple refocusing of vantage point, clears the blurred egocentric lens that questions the Father's love and motive for chastisement. Captivity serves as the Israelites (and our) chance to view their transgressions as the Father has seen them. It is difficult to see one's wickedness, but watching it play out before you is 20/20. The same way Yahuah watched as the Israelites caused their children to pass through the fire, committed spiritual adultery, whored their children, and all the other transgressions that placed them in this position is how they are now forced to watch it play out before their own eyes. Yahuah is not *witnessing* the mistreatment in a literal sense, because he has already seen it. Instead, He is allowing His children to see what He has seen and is making them live out what they have asked for. The same thing that seemed like pleasure at one's owns hands is a nightmare in the hands of the oppressor. In captivity, Yahuah purges through close interaction with sin to give His children a front row seat to their sin so that they will not do it again. The grace and mercy of the Father is that He designates the end of chastisement and gives restoration and peace as the reward for rebalancing and enduring His drawing out process. But just as Yah turned His back as the Messiah hung for restitution (to reconcile or bring *Shalom*), He has also set an appointed end for captivity; but He must turn to allow the completion of His restoration at every level. Due to the curses that the children of Israel heaped upon themselves in the promised land they had to be removed, taken into captivity, cleansed, and then the land and the people can be joined in shalom unto the Father!

> *For I know the thoughts that I think toward you, saith Yahuah, thoughts of peace, and not of evil, to give you an expected end. Then shall ye call upon me, and ye shall go and pray unto me, and I will hearken unto you. And ye shall seek me, and find me when ye shall search for me with all your heart. And I will be found of you, saith Yahuah: and I will turn away your captivity, and I will gather you from all the nations, and from all the places whither I have driven you, saith Yahuah; and I will bring you again into the place whence I caused you to be carried away captive.*
> **Jeremiah 29:11-14**

STUDY TWO

---

# Matrix: Rechem (רחם)

*That thou shalt set apart unto Yahuah all that openeth the matrix, and every firstling that cometh of a beast which thou hast; the males shall be Yahuah's.*
**Exodus 13:12**

In the blockbuster movie, the Matrix, there is a scene where the main character Neo is confronted with the reality of the matrix. From within the matrix, he is made aware that his reality is a simulated experience controlled by a greater force. He must decide to come out. But by merely desiring to get out he faces issues. It was not until his desire met adversity that the subconscious part of him was birthed and he was made alive. In scripture, the birthing process is referred to as passing through the matrix. It is this process of passing through that makes us alive, but it is not what makes man live. Understanding the connection between the process of birthing and the process of awakening is critical. Three major Hebrew words are used to show the stages of the womb and the birth of the subconscious to a physical form. By studying and meditating on these words and definitions, you will have the opportunity to experience the beauty of your body as a vehicle of divine manifestation as well as the portal through which the intentions of another are made manifest. Each word gives the stage of the womb and shows the importance of the "portal" called the woman.

# ☥⊙〰

מעה (M-AhH) Strong's #4577, 4578/ AHLB #1292

A hidden thing that only Yah knows
An unknown that is known by a higher consciousness
Gut or lower region
Seat of Consciousness
Internal organs of the lower torso


*And, behold, the word of Yahuah came unto him,
saying, this shall not be thine heir; but he that
shall come forth out of thine own **bowels** shall be
thine heir.*

וְהִנֵּ֨ה דְבַר־יְהוָ֤ה אֵלָיו֙ לֵאמֹ֔ר לֹ֥א
יִֽירָשְׁךָ֖ זֶ֑ה כִּי־אִם֙ אֲשֶׁ֣ר יֵצֵ֣א
**מִמֵּעֶ֔יךָ** ה֖וּא יִֽירָשֶֽׁךָ

Genesis 15:4

# ⵡ⊗🗆

בטן (BThN) Strong's #990/ AHLB #2015

Pistachio
Protruding stomach
Rounded projection
House which surrounds the seed
Growing belly due to seed inside

*And Jacob's anger was kindled against Rachel: and he said, Am I in Elohim's stead, who hath withheld from thee the fruit of the **womb**?*

וַיִּחַר־אַף יַעֲקֹב בְּרָחֵל וַיֹּאמֶר
הֲתַחַת אֱלֹהִים אָנֹכִי אֲשֶׁר־מָנַע
מִמֵּךְ פְּרִי־**בָטֶן**

Genesis 30:2

𐤓𐤄𐤌

**רחם** (R-Hhm) Strong's #7358/ AHLB #2762

The head separated by water
Compassion
Maiden
First born

*That thou shalt set apart unto Yahuah all that openeth the **matrix**, and every firstling that cometh of a beast which thou hast; the males shall be Yahuah's.*

וְהַעֲבַרְתָּ כָל־פֶּטֶר־**רֶחֶם**
לַיהֹוָה וְכָל־פֶּטֶר ׀ שֶׁגֶר בְּהֵמָה
אֲשֶׁר יִהְיֶה לְךָ הַזְּכָרִים לַיהֹוָה׃

Exodus 13:12

## Application

The womb, seed, and Yah are all a part of a triune covenant. Yah guides the subconscious and the desire. The man gives the physical seed, and the woman takes the subconscious will of the father and the desire of the male and manifests a child that will be nurtured and given back to the one who knew he or she before they were even knit in the womb. Three forms of the womb with one (Echad) purpose.

> *As for me, behold, my covenant is with thee, and thou shalt be a father of many nations. Neither shall thy name any more be called Abram, but thy name shall be Abraham; for a father of many nations have I made thee. And I will make thee exceeding fruitful, and I will make nations of thee, and kings shall come out of thee. And I will establish my covenant between me and thee and thy seed after thee in their generations for an everlasting covenant, to be a Elohim unto thee, and to thy seed after thee. And Yah said unto Abraham, As for Sarai thy wife, thou shalt not call her name Sarai, but Sarah shall her name be. And I will bless her, and give thee a son also of her: yea, I will bless her, and she shall be a mother of nations; kings of people shall be of her.*
>
> Gen 17:4-7;15-16

# Submit: Anah (ענה)

*Submitting yourselves one to another in the fear of YAH.*
**Ephesians 5:21**

<u>ענה</u> (AhNH) Strong's #6031,6033 / AHLB #1359

Watch intently

Concentrate

Humble

Be occupied or busied with

To be in a position that makes one look up

*And the angel of Yahuah said unto her, Return to thy mistress, and __submit__ thyself under her hands.*

ג וַיֹּאמֶר לָהֹ מַלְאַךְ יְהוָֹה שׁוּבִי
אֶל־גְּבִרְתֵּךְ **וְהִתְעַנִּי** תַּחַת יָדֶיהָ
Genesis 16:9

13

## כחש (KHhSh) Strong's #3584, 3585,3586/ AHLB #2257

Pretend obedience

To correct

Deny justified demands

To withhold something to get a desired outcome

Withholding to cause leanness

To withhold what you have in your hand to afflict another

*Then Sarah **denied**, saying, I laughed not; for she was afraid. And he said, Nay; but thou didst laugh.*

וַתְּכַחֵשׁ שָׂרָה ׀ לֵאמֹר לֹא צָחַקְתִּי
כִּי ׀ יָרֵאָה וַיֹּאמֶר ׀ לֹא כִּי צָחָקְתְּ

Genesis 18:15

## רפס (RPS) Strong's #7511,7512,7515/ AHLB #2786

Stomping down

The head trampling or stomping with speech

Impoverish or lower

Cause to cover

control

Rebuke the company of spearmen, the multitude of the bulls, with the calves of the people, *till every one* **submit** himself with pieces of
silver: scatter thou the people *that* delight in war.

גְּעַ֨ר חַיַּ֪ת קָנֶ֡ה עֲדַ֨ת אַבִּירִ֤ים ׀
בְּעֶגְלֵ֬י עַמִּ֗ים **מִתְרַפֵּ֥ס** בְּרַצֵּי־
כָ֑סֶף בִּזַּ֥ר עַמִּ֗ים קְרָב֥וֹת יֶחְפָּֽצוּ

Psalm 68:30

---

# Build: Banah (בנה)

*That thou shalt set apart unto Yahuah all that openeth the matrix, and every firstling that cometh of a beast which thou hast; the males shall be Yahuah's.*

**Exodus 13:12**

בנה (B-NH) Strong's #1124, 1129/ AHLB #1037

Forming

Having children

Producer

Endowing

Structure built for occupation

Repairer

Builder


*Then the rib which Yahuah Elohim had taken from man He **made** into a woman, and He brought her to the man.*

וַיִּ֩בֶן֩ יְהֹוָ֨ה אֱלֹהִ֧ים ׀ אֶֽת־הַצֵּלָ֛ע
אֲשֶׁר־לָקַ֥ח מִן־הָֽאָדָ֖ם לְאִשָּׁ֑ה
וַיְבִאֶ֖הָ אֶל־הָֽאָדָֽם

Genesis 2:22

# פֿשׂלֿ

בון (BWN) Strong's #8394/ AHLB #1037

Intelligence

The skill of mind and hands

Planning and building of a house

Mediate

Consider

Teacher

*So that you incline your ear to wisdom, and apply your heart to __understanding__;*

לְהַקְשִׁ֣יב לַחׇכְמָ֣ה אׇזְנֶ֑ךָ תַּטֶּ֥ה
לִ֝בְּךָ֗ **לַתְּבוּנָֽה**

Proverbs 2:2

__בנן__ (BNN) Strong's #1146,1147/ AHLB #1037

Building or housing a family

The structure that houses the family

The continuing of the house requires a womb and a seed

*Now there was a wall around the outside of the temple. In the man's hand was a measuring rod six cubits long, each being a cubit and a hand-breadth; and he measure the width of the wall* **structure**, *one rod; and height, one rod.*

וְהִנֵּה חוֹמָה מִחוּץ לַבַּיִת סָבִיב ׀
סָבִיב וּבְיַד הָאִישׁ קְנֵה הַמִּדָּה שֵׁשׁ־
אַמּוֹת בָּאַמָּה וָטֹפַח וַיָּמָד אֶת־רֹחַב
__הַבִּנְיָן__ קָנֶה אֶחָד וְקוֹמָה קָנֶה אֶחָד׃

Ezekiel 40:5

__בין__ (BYN) Strong's #995,996,997,998,999,1143/ AHLB #1037

Understand

Discernment between two things or sides

Having insight

Revealing or making known
Understanding interactions of elements

*Now therefore, let Pharaoh select a **discerning** and wise man, and set him over the land of Egypt.*

וְעַתָּה יֵרֶא פַרְעֹה אִישׁ **נָבוֹן** וְחָכָם
וִישִׁיתֵהוּ עַל־אֶרֶץ מִצְרָיִם

Genesis 41:33

פנה (PN-Kh) Strong's #6847,6437,3942,6440/ AHLB #1382

Safe guarding
Join elements

And Pharaoh called Joseph's name Zaphnath-**Paaneah**.

וַיִּקְרָא פַרְעֹה שֵׁם־יוֹסֵף צָפְנַת
**פַּעְנֵחַ** וַיִּתֶּן־לוֹ אֶת־אָסְנַת בַּת־פּוֹטִי
פֶרַע כֹּהֵן אֹן לְאִשָּׁה וַיֵּצֵא יוֹסֵף עַל־
אֶרֶץ מִצְרָיִם

Genesis 41:45

## STUDY FIVE

---

# Family: Shapach (שפח)

*But if any provide not for his own, and specially for those of his own house,*
*he hath denied the faith, and is worse than an infidel.*
**1 Timothy 5:8**

שפח (ShPHh) Strong's #8198,4940/ AHLB #2863

Family

Join to a maiden

Increase by attaching

A female who gives her body to serve in building a clan

*But you shall go to my father's house and to my*
**family**, *and take a wife for my son.*

אִם־לֹא אֶל־בֵּית־אָבִי תֵּלֵךְ וְאֶל־
**מִשְׁפַּחְתִּי** וְלָקַחְתָּ אִשָּׁה לִבְנִי

Genesis 24:38

# ✝◣◻†

**בית** (BYT) Strong's #1004,1005/ AHLB #1045

House
Place of protection
Family mark
Tribe
People
 Nest
Jail
Grave

*Then Yahuah said to Noah, "Come into the ark, you and all your **household**, because I have seen that you are righteous before Me in this generation.*

וַיֹּאמֶר יְהוָה֙ לְנֹ֔חַ בֹּֽא־אַתָּ֥ה וְכָל־ **בֵּֽיתְךָ֖** אֶל־הַתֵּבָ֑ה כִּֽי־אֹתְךָ֥ רָאִ֛יתִי צַדִּ֥יק לְפָנַ֖י בַּדּ֥וֹר הַזֶּֽה

Genesis 7:1

**טפף** (ThPP) Strong's #2952,2945/ AHLB #1201
Unsteady steps

The skipping or stumbling of children

*Moreover your **little ones**, which ye said should be a prey, and your children, which in that day had no knowledge between good and evil, they shall go in thither, and unto them will I give it, and they shall possess it.*

וְטַפְּכֶם אֲשֶׁר אֲמַרְתֶּם לָבַז יִהְיֶה וּבְנֵיכֶם אֲשֶׁר לֹא־יָדְעוּ הַיּוֹם טוֹב וָרָע הֵמָּה יָבֹאוּ שָׁמָּה וְלָהֶם אֶתְּנֶנָּה וְהֵם יִירָשׁוּהָ

Deuteronomy 1:39

אלף (ALP) Strong's #441 / AHLB #2001
Guide
Yoke
Receive from others
Lack independence
Leader whose followers are dependent

*But it was thou, a man mine equal, my **guide**, and mine acquaintance.*

וְאַתָּה אֱנוֹשׁ כְּעֶרְכִּי אַלּוּפִי וּמְיֻדָּעִי

Psalm 55:13

# Woman: Isha (אשה)

**אשה** (AShH) Strong's #801,802/ AHLB #1021

Foundation
Black
Strong pressing down
Fire shaped material
Supporting pillar
Created material

*And if the **woman** is not willing to follow you, then you will be released from tis oath; do not take my son back there.*

וְאִם־לֹא תֹאבֶה הָ**אִשָּׁה** לָלֶכֶת
אַחֲרֶיךָ וְנִקִּיתָ מִשְּׁבֻעָתִי זֹאת רַק
אֶת־בְּנִי לֹא תָשֵׁב שמה

Genesis 24:8

# גֻ שׁ יׁ

נשה (NSh) Strong's #5382/ AHLB #1320

Continually pressing

A debt or deception which causes oppression

Obligate

Give up rights

Submitting

More delicate sex

Cause to forget

*Joseph called the name of the first-born Manasseh: "For Yah has made me **forget** all my toil and all my father's house."*

וַיִּקְרָא יוֹסֵף אֶת־שֵׁם הַבְּכוֹר
**מְנַשֶּׁה** כִּי־נַשַּׁנִי אֱלֹהִים אֶת־כָּל־
עֲמָלִי וְאֵת כָּל־בֵּית אָבִי

Genesis 41:51

נקב (NQB) Strong's #5344,5345,5347 / AHLB #1416,2430

hole

Designated one

Appoint

To make whole in order to deposit
To place a ring or hole in
*Then Jehoiada the priest took a chest, bored a* **hole** *in its lid, and set it beside the altar, on the right side as one comes into the house of Ya-huah; and the priests who kept the door put there all the money brought into the house of Ya-huah.*

וַיִּקַּח יְהוֹיָדָע הַכֹּהֵן אֲרוֹן אֶחָד
**וַיִּקֹּב** חֹר בְּדַלְתּוֹ וַיִּתֵּן אֹתוֹ אֵצֶל
הַמִּזְבֵּחַ [בַּיָּמִין כ] (מִיָּמִין ק)
בְּבוֹא־אִישׁ בֵּית יְהֹוָה וְנָתְנוּ־שָׁמָּה
הַכֹּהֲנִים שֹׁמְרֵי הַסַּף אֶת־כָּל־
הַכֶּסֶף הַמּוּבָא בֵית־יְהֹוָה

2 Kings 12:9

# Man: Zakar (זכר)

זכר (NSh) Strong's #234, 1798-9,2142-3,2145-6/ AHLB #1320

Remember

Historian

Mindful

Mention through speech

Speak on the behalf of another

Speak for the family

*Three times in the year all thy **males** shall appear before Yahuah ELOHIM.*

שָׁלֹשׁ פְּעָמִים בַּשָּׁנָה יֵרָאֶה֙ כָּל־
**זְכוּרְךָ֔** אֶל־פְּנֵי הָאָדֹן ׀ יְהוָֽה

Exodus 23:17

# 𐤍𐤅𐤁

**בֵּן** (BN) Strong's #1121,1123,1247/ AHLB #1037

Continuing of the house

Lasting

Seed of the house

And Abraham circumcised his **son** Isaac being eight days **old**, as Elohim had commanded him.

וַיָּ֤מָל אַבְרָהָם֙ אֶת־יִצְחָ֣ק **בְּנ֔וֹ בֶּן**־ שְׁמֹנַ֖ת יָמִ֑ים כַּאֲשֶׁ֛ר צִוָּ֥ה אֹת֖וֹ אֱלֹהִֽים

Genesis 21:4

**אָדָם** (A-DM) Strong's #119,120/ AHLB #1082

Ground

Earthy

Likeness

Flowing of Blood

Rich in Minerals

Mankind

*And Elohim said, Let us make **man** in our image, after our likeness: and let them have dominion over the fish of the sea, and over the fowl of the*

*air, and over the cattle, and over all the earth, and*
*over every creeping thing that creepeth upon the*
*earth.*

וַיֹּ֣אמֶר אֱלֹהִים נַֽעֲשֶׂ֤ה **אָדָם**
בְּצַלְמֵ֖נוּ כִּדְמוּתֵ֑נוּ וְיִרְדּוּ֩ בִדְגַ֨ת הַיָּ֜ם
וּבְע֣וֹף הַשָּׁמַ֗יִם וּבַבְּהֵמָה֙ וּבְכָל־הָאָ֔רֶץ
וּבְכָל־הָרֶ֖מֶשׂ הָֽרֹמֵ֥שׂ עַל־הָאָֽרֶץ

Genesis 1:26

א**ִישׁ** (AYSh) Strong's #376,380/ AHLB #1021
Charred after being burned in fire
fire
black
black of night
pillar
man with proven character

*And Adam knew Eve his wife; and she conceived,*
*and bare Cain, and said, I have gotten a **man***
*from Yahuah.*

וְהָ֣אָדָ֔ם יָדַ֖ע אֶת־חַוָּ֣ה אִשְׁתּ֑וֹ וַתַּ֛הַר וַתֵּ֥לֶד
אֶת־קַ֨יִן֙ וַתֹּ֔אמֶר קָנִ֥יתִי **אִישׁ** אֶת־יְהוָֽה

Genesis 4:1

**גבר** (GBR) Strong's #1396/ AHLB #2052

Authority

Prevail

Warrior

Control through physical strength

Overpower

Victorious

Master

Strong

And Cush begat Nimrod: he began to be a **mighty** one in the earth.

וְכוּשׁ יָלַד אֶת־נִמְרֹד הוּא הֵחֵל
לִהְיוֹת **גִּבֹּר** בָּאָרֶץ

Genesis 10:8

---

# Queen: Sarah (שרה/סרה)

𐤔𐤀𐤓𐤔

שרה/סרה (S-RH) Strong's #8283/ AHLB #1342

Nobel woman
Turning heads (people)
Exerting Superior Power
Supporting the head
Turn the leaders to Yah
Revolt

*And Elohim said unto Abraham, As for Sarai thy wife, thou shalt not call her name Sarai, but* **Sarah** *shall her name be.*

וַיֹּאמֶר אֱלֹהִים אֶל־אַבְרָהָם שָׂרַי
אִשְׁתְּךָ לֹא־תִקְרָא אֶת־שְׁמָהּ שָׂרַי
כִּי **שָׂרָה** שְׁמָהּ
Genesis 17:15

# †山ᗐ/ᗰ

**מלכת** (ML-KH) Strong's #4433,4436/ AHLB #2340

Advising

Counsel

Consult

Of the people

Walking among the people

*And the thing was known to Mordecai, who told it unto Esther the **queen**; and Esther certified the king thereof in Mordecai's name.*

וַיִּוָּדַע הַדָּבָר֙ לְמָרְדֳּכַ֔י וַיַּגֵּד
לְאֶסְתֵּר **הַמַּלְכָּה** וַתֹּאמֶר אֶסְתֵּר
לַמֶּלֶךְ בְּשֵׁם מָרְדֳּכָי

Esther 2:22

# Virtuous: Chayil (חיל)

*Who can find a virtuous woman? for her price is far above rubies.*

**Proverbs 31:10**

חיל (HhYL) Strong's #2426,2427,2428,2429,2430/ AHLB #1173
Power
A hole through which the enemy enters a city
Strength and wealth of a person
bulwark

*Mark ye well her **bulwarks**, consider her palaces;*
*that ye may tell it to the generation following.*

וְשִׁיתוּ לִבְּכֶם ׀ **לְחֵילָה** פַּסְּגוּ
אַרְמְנוֹתֶיהָ לְמַעַן תְּסַפְּרוּ לְדוֹר
אַחֲרוֹן

Psalm 48:13

---

# Mother: Em (אם)

## אם(מ)ם (AM) Strong's #517,519,520,521/ AHLB #1013

Be dependent

Point of Departure

Arm

Bind

Glue

The arms that hold things together

Strong water

Giving physical and spiritual life

*And Adam called his wife's name Eve; because she was the **mother** of all living.*

וַיִּקְרָא הָאָדָם שֵׁם אִשְׁתּוֹ חַוָּה כִּי
הִוא הָיְתָה **אֵם** כָּל־חָי

Genesis 3:20

אמה (A-MH) Strong's #517,519,520,521/ AHLB #1013

Serve

Pillar

Bondwoman

Support

*Wherefore she said unto Abraham, Cast out this **bondwoman** and her son: for the son of this bondwoman shall not be heir with my son, even with Isaac.*

וַתֹּאמֶר לְאַבְרָהָם גָּרֵשׁ **הָאָמָה**
הַזֹּאת וְאֶת־בְּנָהּ כִּי לֹא יִירַשׁ בֶּן־
הָאָמָה הַזֹּאת עִם־בְּנִי עִם־יִצְחָק

Genesis 21:10

---

# Help: Azar (עזר)

*Whoso findeth a wife findeth a good thing, and obtaineth favour of the Yah.*
**Proverbs 18:22**

**עזר** (AhZR) Strong's #5826,5828,5833/ AHLB #2535

Restrian

Support

Ally

Progress

Help to reduce responsibilities

Gird

*And Yahuah Elohim said, It is not good that the man should be alone; I will make him an **help meet** for him.*

וַיֹּאמֶר יְהוָה אֱלֹהִים לֹא־טוֹב הֱיוֹת הָאָדָם לְבַדּוֹ אֶעֱשֶׂה־לּוֹ **עֵזֶר** כְּנֶגְדּוֹ

Genesis 2:18

# Rib: Tsela (צלע)

צלע (Ts-LAh) Strong's #5967,6760,6761,6763/ AHLB #2664

Surrounding wall

Side

Limp

Fall

Favoring one side

Beam

*And the **rib**, which Yahuah Elohim had taken from man, made he a woman, and brought her unto the man.*

וַיִּבֶן יְהֹוָה אֱלֹהִים ׀ אֶת־**הַצֵּלָע**
אֲשֶׁר־לָקַח מִן־הָאָדָם לְאִשָּׁה
וַיְבִאֶהָ אֶל־הָאָדָם

Genesis 2:22

## STUDY THIRTEEN

---

# Deceived: Nasha (נשה)

And Adam was not deceived, but the woman being deceived was in the transgression.
**1 Timothy 2:14**

נשה (NSh) Strong's #4860,4855,5383,5386/ AHLB #1320

Loan

Debt

Deception

Pressing the seed

Beguile

*The enemy shall not **exact** upon him; nor the son of wickedness afflict him.*

לֹא־**יַשִּׁא** אוֹיֵב בּוֹ וּבֶן־עַוְלָה לֹא יְעַנֶּנּוּ

Psalm 89:22

# 𐤔𐤋𐤋𐤔(𐤀𐤙)

שגג(ה) (ShG) Strong's #4870,4879,7683-4,7686 / AHLB #1436

Sin

Err

To cause to repeat

Double burden

Error made on accident or unintentionally

Careless mistake

*And if ye have **erred**, and not observed all these commandments, which Yahuah hath spoken unto Moses*

וְכִי **תִשְׁגּוּ** וְלֹא תַעֲשׂוּ אֵת כָּל־
הַמִּצְוֹת הָאֵלֶּה אֲשֶׁר־דִּבֶּר יְהוָה
אֶל־מֹשֶׁה

Numbers 15:22

# 𐤔𐤙𐤕𐤋

התל (H-TL) Strong's #2048,4123/ AHLB #1495

Debt that causes oppression

To hang

Deflate

Mock

*And Delilah said unto Samson, Behold, thou hast* **mocked** *me, and told me lies: now tell me, I pray thee, wherewith thou mightest be bound.*

וַתֹּ֤אמֶר דְּלִילָה֙ אֶל־שִׁמְשׁ֔וֹן הִנֵּה֙ **הֵתַ֣לְתָּ** בִּ֔י וַתְּדַבֵּ֥ר אֵלַ֖י כְּזָבִ֑ים עַתָּה֙ הַגִּֽידָה־נָּ֣א לִ֔י בַּמֶּ֖ה תֵּאָסֵֽר

Judges 16:10

STUDY FOURTEEN

# Meek: Anav (עָנָו)
# &
# Quiet: Shataq (שָׁתַק)

Whose adorning let it not be that outward adorning of plaiting the hair, and

of wearing of gold, or of putting on of apparel; But let it be the hidden man

of the heart, in that which is not corruptible, even the ornament of a meek

and quiet spirit, which is in the sight of God of great price.

**1 Peter 3:3-4**

עָנָו (Ah-NW) Strong's #6035,6037-8/ AHLB #1359

For the sake of

Sate of poverty

Lowliness

Gentle

Guarding something of importance

Watching and willing to die for the seed

Experienced and secured to the seed

Oppressed

*(Now the man Moses was very **meek**, above all the men which were upon the face of the earth.)*

וְהָאִישׁ מֹשֶׁה [**עָנָו** כ] (**עָנָיו** ק) מְאֹד מִכֹּל הָאָדָם אֲשֶׁר עַל־פְּנֵי הָאֲדָמָה

Number 12:3

**‑ө‑†ɯ**

שתק (ShTQ) Strong's #8367,120/ AHLB #2889

Silence

Still

Calming

Satisfying rightful need

*Then are they glad because they be **quiet**; so he bringeth them unto their desired haven.*

וַיִּשְׂמְחוּ כִי־**יִשְׁתֹּקוּ** וַיַּנְחֵם אֶל־מְחוֹז חֶפְצָם

Psalm 107:30

# YᘓШ

שׁלו (ShLW) Strong's #7951,7959,7961-3,/ AHLB #1021

Prosper

Drawing out what is needed

Assur

Being complete

Undisturbed peace

placenta

*Peace be within thy walls, and **prosperity** within thy palaces.*

יְהִי־**שָׁלוֹם** בְּחֵילֵךְ לְוָה בְּאַרְמְנוֹתָיִךְ

Psalm 122:7

רגע (GBR) Strong's #7280-2,4774/ AHLB #2752

Restrain

Cease movement

Careful movement

Stir up from rest

The moving of water

Wink of an eye

refreshing

*And among these nations shalt thou find no* **ease**, *neither shall the sole of thy foot have rest: but Yahuah shall give thee there a trembling heart, and failing of eyes, and sorrow of mind.*

וּבַגּוֹיִם הָהֵם֙ לֹ֣א **תַרְגִּ֔יעַ** וְלֹא־
יִהְיֶ֥ה מָנ֖וֹחַ לְכַף־רַגְלֶ֑ךָ וְנָתַן֩ יְהֹוָ֨ה לְךָ֜
שָׁם֙ לֵ֣ב רַגָּ֔ז וְכִלְי֥וֹן עֵינַ֖יִם וְדַֽאֲב֥וֹן נָֽפֶשׁ

Deuteronomy 28:65

שָׁאַן (ShAN) Strong's #7599/ AHLB #1474

Separation

Sharpen

Rest

Fortunate

protected

*Our soul is exceedingly filled with the scorning* **of those that are at ease**, *and with the contempt of the proud.*

רַבַּת֙ שָֽׂבְעָה־לָּ֣הּ נַפְשֵׁ֔נוּ הַלַּ֖עַג
**הַשַּׁאֲנַנִּ֑ים** הַבּ֖וּז לִגְאֵיוֹנִֽים

Psalm 123:4

## STUDY FIFTEEN

---

# Keeper: Shamar (שמר)

Here is the patience of the saints: here are they that keep the commandments of Yahuah, and the faith of Yahusha.

**Revelations 14:12**

שמר (ShMR) Strong's #8104-5,8108/ AHLB #2853

Protect

Keep from danger

Guard

Save life

Preserve

Watchman

Being aware

Building a protected wall around

*Only take heed to thyself, and **keep** thy soul diligently, lest thou forget the things which thine eyes have seen, and lest they depart from thy heart all the days of thy life: but teach them thy sons, and thy sons' sons;*

רַק הִשָּׁמֶר לְךָ וּשְׁמֹר נַפְשְׁךָ
מְאֹד פֶּן־תִּשְׁכַּח אֶת־הַדְּבָרִים
אֲשֶׁר־רָאוּ עֵינֶיךָ וּפֶן־יָסוּרוּ
מִלְּבָבְךָ כֹּל יְמֵי חַיֶּיךָ וְהוֹדַעְתָּם
לְבָנֶיךָ וְלִבְנֵי בָנֶיךָ

Deuteronomy 4:9

<u>נטר</u> (NThR) Strong's #5201,5202/ AHLB #2400

Protecting

Maintain

Grudge

*He will not always chide: neither will he* **keep** *his anger for ever.*

לֹא־לָנֶצַח יָרִיב וְלֹא לְעוֹלָם <u>יִטּוֹר</u>

Psalm 107:30

<u>נצר</u> (NTsR) Strong's #5341,5341/ AHLB #2429

A pressing in or on something

To close in with pressure

Watching

Controlling

Protected bud- guarding the seed as it grows

Branch

Movement

Hidden thing

*And there shall come forth a rod out of the stem of Jesse, and a **Branch** shall grow out of his roots:*

יֵצֵא חֹטֶר מִגֵּזַע יִשָׁי **וְנֵצֶר** מִשָּׁרָשָׁיו יִפְרֶה

Isaiah 11:1

# Crown: Ketar (עטר)

# שׁ+אֿ

כתר (KTR) Strong's #3803-5/ AHLB #2300

To surround

Encircle

Crown

Top of a pillar as a crown

Place a sign or covenant on the head

Royal covenant

*And the king loved Esther above all the women, and she obtained grace and favour in his sight more than all the virgins; so that he set the royal* **crown** *upon her head, and made her queen instead of Vashti.*

וַיֶּאֱהַב הַמֶּלֶךְ אֶת־אֶסְתֵּר מִכָּל־הַנָּשִׁים
וַתִּשָּׂא־חֵן וָחֶסֶד לְפָנָיו מִכָּל־הַבְּתוּלֹת
וַיָּשֶׂם **כֶּתֶר**־מַלְכוּת בְּרֹאשָׁהּ וַיַּמְלִיכֶהָ
תַּחַת וַשְׁתִּי

Esther 2:17

<u>עטר</u> (AhThR) Strong's #5849,5850/ AHLB #2538

To bestow a crown

Encircle

Wreath

Sigh of authority

*Who redeemeth thy life from destruction; who*
**<u>crowneth</u>** *thee with lovingkindness and tender*
*mercies;*

הַגּוֹאֵל מִשַּׁחַת חַיָּיְכִי **<u>הַמְעַטְרֵכִי</u>**
חֶסֶד וְרַחֲמִים

Psalm 103:4

**נזר** (NZR) Strong's #4502,5144,5145/ AHLB #2390

Separate

Warning/ teaching to be set apart

Nazarite

Uncut hair

Consecrate

Dedicate

Woman's hair/ hair

*And thou shalt put the mitre upon his head, and put the holy **crown** upon the mitre.*

ל וְשַׂמְתָּ הַמִּצְנֶפֶת עַל־רֹאשׁוֹ
וְנָתַתָּ אֶת־**נֵזֶר** הַקֹּדֶשׁ עַל־הַמִּצְנָפֶת

Exodus 29:6

STUDY SEVENTEEN

# Roots: Shoresh (שרש)

שרש (ShRSh) Strong's #8327/ AHLB #2883
Connect elements
Take root
To plant and allow to flourish

*Thou preparedst room before it, and didst cause it to **take deep root**, and it filled the land.*

פִּנִּיתָ לְפָנֶיהָ **וַתַּשְׁרֵשׁ** רָשֶׁיהָ
וַתְּמַלֵּא־אָרֶץ Psalm 80:9

נתק (NTQ) Strong's #5423-4,5428/ AHLB #2455
Tear apart
Transplant

Destroy roots
Removal of the seed (covenant)
Pull to a breaking point

**_Let us break their bands asunder_**, *and cast*
*away their cords from us.*

נְנַתְּקָה אֶת־מוֹסְרוֹתֵימוֹ וְנַשְׁלִיכָה
מִמֶּנּוּ עֲבֹתֵימוֹ

Psalm 2:3

נתש (NTSh) Strong's #5428/ AHLB #1321,2456
Uprooting
Pluck
Remove

*And Yahuah* **_rooted them out_** *of their land in*
*anger, and in wrath, and in great indignation,*
*and cast them into another land, as it is this day.*

וַיִּתְּשֵׁם יְהוָֹה מֵעַל אַדְמָתָם
בְּאַף וּבְחֵמָה וּבְקֶצֶף גָּדוֹל
וַיַּשְׁלִכֵם אֶל־אֶרֶץ אַחֶרֶת כַּיּוֹם
הַזֶּה

Deut 29:28

עָקַר (GhQR) Strong's #6133,6135/ AHLB #2905

Barren

Make lame

Impotent

Pull root out of the ground


*He maketh the **barren** woman to keep*
*house, and to be a joyful mother of children.*
*Praise ye Yahuah.*

מוֹשִׁיבִי ׀ **עֲקֶרֶת** הַבַּ֖יִת אֵם־
הַבָּנִים שְׂמֵחָה הַלְלוּ־יָהּ

Psalm 113:9

# Ground: Adamah (אדמה)

**אדם** (ADM) Strong's #126,127,1819,1823-4/ AHLB #1082

Rich in minerals

Yielding sustenance

Tilled

Earth substance for building or constructing

Likeness

Using nutrients from one place to create another

*How shall I give thee up, Ephraim? how shall I deliver thee, Israel? how shall I make thee as* **Admah**? *how shall I set thee as Zeboim? mine heart is turned within me, my repentings are kindled together.*

אֵיךְ אֶתֶּנְךָ אֶפְרַיִם אֲמַגֶּנְךָ
יִשְׂרָאֵל אֵיךְ אֶתֶּנְךָ **כְאַדְמָה**

אֲשִׂימְךָ כִּצְבֹאיִם נֶהְפַּךְ עָלַי לִבִּי
יַחַד נִכְמְרוּ נִחוּמָי

Hosea 11:8

<u>עפר</u> (AhPR) Strong's #6083/ AHLB #2565

Being earthy
Powder
Earth colored

*And Yahuah Elohim formed man of the **dust** of the ground, and breathed into his nostrils the breath of life; and man became a living soul.*

וַיִּיצֶר יְהוָֹה אֱלֹהִים אֶת־
הָאָדָם **עָפָר** מִן־הָאֲדָמָה וַיִּפַּח
בְּאַפָּיו נִשְׁמַת חַיִּים וַיְהִי הָאָדָם
לְנֶפֶשׁ חַיָּה

Genesis 2:7

<u>ש/סהד</u> (SHD) Strong's #7717/ AHLB #1326

Testify/ Testimony

A portion of ground for planting or setting up tents
A place for building structure
Field
Foundation
Level place
Record that lays a foundation about an event

*Also now, behold, my witness is in heaven,* **and**
**my record** *is on high.*

גַּם־עַתָּה הִנֵּה־בַשָּׁמַיִם עֵדִי
וְֽשָׂהֲדִי בַּמְּרוֹמִים

Job 16:19

עוּר (AhWR) Strong's #5783-5,6174/ AHLB #2905

See a man
Covering for the soul
Brilliance
Glow or burn
Awakening
Naked
Skin
Blind

*And they were both **naked**, the man and his wife, and were not ashamed.*

וַיִּהְיוּ שְׁנֵיהֶם֙ **עֲרוּמִּים** הָֽאָדָ֖ם
וְאִשְׁתּ֑וֹ וְלֹ֖א יִתְבֹּשָֽׁשׁוּ

Genesis 2:25

STUDY NINETEEN

# Truth: Emet (אמת)

Yahusha saith unto him, I am the way, the truth, and the life: no man cometh
unto the Father, but by me.

**John 14:6**

מנה (M-NH) Strong's #4490/ AHLB #1290

Kind

Portion

Allocation

Belong

Collection

*Yahuah is the **portion** of mine inheritance and of*
*my cup: thou maintainest my lot.*

יְהֹוָה **מְנָת**־חֶלְקִי וְכוֹסִי אַתָּה
תּוֹמִיךְ גּוֹרָלִי

Psalm 16:5

<u>אמן</u> (AMN) Strong's #539/ AHLB #1290

Sure

Seed

Depend upon

Rely on

Affirmation

Stand firm

Strength through blood

Faithful

*And the people **believed**: and when they heard that Yahuah had visited the children of Israel, and that he had looked upon their affliction, then they bowed their heads and worshipped.*

וַיַּֽאֲמֵ֖ן הָעָ֑ם וַֽיִּשְׁמְע֡וּ כִּֽי־פָקַ֣ד
יְהוָ֣ה אֶת־בְּנֵ֣י יִשְׂרָאֵל֒ וְכִ֣י רָאָה֙
אֶת־עָנְיָ֔ם וַֽיִּקְּד֖וּ וַיִּֽשְׁתַּחֲוֻֽוּ

Exodus 4:31

<u>נצב</u> (NTsB) Strong's #5324/ AHLB #2426

Stand/ Wall

Protecting against harsh elements
Stem of a tree
Fixed
Enduring
Erect

*And, behold, Yahuah **stood** above it, and said,*
*I am Yahuah Elohim of Abraham thy father, and*
*the Elohim of Isaac: the land whereon thou liest,*
*to thee will I give it, and to thy seed;*

וְהִנֵּה יְהֹוָה֙ **נִצָּב** עָלָיו֮ וַיֹּאמַ֔ר
אֲנִי יְהֹוָה֙ אֱלֹהֵי֙ אַבְרָהָ֣ם אָבִ֔יךָ
וֵאלֹהֵי יִצְחָ֑ק הָאָ֗רֶץ אֲשֶׁ֤ר אַתָּה֙
שֹׁכֵ֣ב עָלֶ֔יהָ לְךָ֥ אֶתְּנֶ֖נָּה וּלְזַרְעֶֽךָ

Genesis 28:13

אמנה (A-MW-NH) Strong's #530,4327,4480-1/ AHLB #1290
Stability
What is firm
What is true about an individual
Where a person is from

*But Moses' hands were heavy; and they took a*
*stone, and put it under him, and he sat thereon;*

*and Aaron and Hur stayed up his hands, the one
on the one side, and the other on the other side;
and his hands were **steady** until the going down
of the sun.*

וִידֵי מֹשֶׁה֙ כְּבֵדִ֔ים וַיִּקְחוּ־אֶ֨בֶן
וַיָּשִׂ֤ימוּ תַחְתָּיו֙ וַיֵּ֣שֶׁב עָלֶ֔יהָ וְאַהֲרֹ֨ן
וְח֜וּר תָּֽמְכ֣וּ בְיָדָ֗יו מִזֶּ֤ה אֶחָד֙ וּמִזֶּ֣ה
אֶחָ֔ד וַיְהִ֥י יָדָ֛יו **אֱמוּנָ֖ה** עַד־בֹּ֥א
הַשָּֽׁמֶשׁ

Exodus 17:12

## ⏦ᘃ⊔ᘁᘔ

<u>קשט</u> (QShTh) Strong's #7189/ AHLB #2739
Weigh
Balance/ Fair
Scale
Outer self
Moral truth
Covenant
Lasting
Caring for

That I might make thee know the **certainty** of
the words of truth; that thou mightest answer
the words of truth to them that send unto thee?

לְהוֹדִיעֲךָ֗ **קֹ֫שְׁט** אִמְרֵי אֱמֶ֑ת
לְהָשִׁ֥יב אֲמָרִ֥ים אֱמֶ֗ת לְשֹׁלְחֶ֥יךָ

Proverbs 22:21

## STUDY TWENTY

# Pregnant: Harah (הרה)

50        200  5

ן ו י ר   ה

6   10

=271

Hebrew word for pregnancy is *herayon* with a gematria of 271 (Strongs #2032)

הר (HR) Strong's #2022/ AHLB #1112

High

Hill

Mountain raising out of the ground

Thou shalt bring them in, and plant them in the
**mountain** of thine inheritance, *in* the place, O

LORD, *which* thou hast made for thee to dwell in, *in* the Sanctuary, O Lord, *which* thy hands have established.

תְּבִאֵמוֹ וְתִטָּעֵמוֹ **בְּהַר**
נַחֲלָתְךָ מָכוֹן לְשִׁבְתְּךָ פָּעַלְתָּ
יְהוָה מִקְּדָשׁ אֲדֹנָי כּוֹנְנוּ יָדֶיךָ

Exodus 15:17

הרה (HRH) Strong's #2029/ AHLB #1112
Source of instruction
Implant and absorb seed
Conceive a child

And Adam knew Eve his wife; and she **conceived**, and bare Cain, and said, I have gotten a man from Yahuah.

וְהָאָדָם יָדַע אֶת־חַוָּה אִשְׁתּוֹ
**וַתַּהַר** וַתֵּלֶד אֶת־קַיִן וַתֹּאמֶר קָנִיתִי
אִישׁ אֶת־יְהוָה

Genesis 4:1

---

# Trust/Refuge: Batach (בטח)

Trust in Yahuah with all thine heart; and lean not unto thine own understanding.

**Proverbs 3:5**

## חסה (HhSH) Strong's #2347,2620,3187,4268/ AHLB #1176

Trust

Look forward to with confidence

Support shelter

Spare

The history of ones family


And he shall say, Where *are* their
gods, *their* rock in whom they **trusted**,

וַיֹּאמַר אֵי אֱלֹהֵימוֹ צוּר **חָסָיוּ** בוֹ

Deuteronomy 32:37

# ⊞⊡⊗⊡⊞

## בטח (BThHh) Strong's #982,983/ AHLB #2013

Feeling secure

Melon protected by thick rind

Confidence

Cling

He **trusted** in the LORD God of Israel; so that after him was none like him among all the kings of Judah, nor *any* that were before him.

וְאַחֲרָיו **בָּטַח** אֱלֹהֵי־יִשְׂרָאֵל בַּיהוָה
יְהוּדָה מַלְכֵי בְּכֹל כָּמֹהוּ לֹא־הָיָה
לְפָנָיו הָיוּ וַאֲשֶׁר

2 Kings 18:5

# Discretion: Sekel

# (שכל/סכל)

As a jewel of gold in a swine's snout, so is a fair woman which is without discretion.

**Proverbs 11:22**

# ﬩ﬠﬥﬤ

**שׂ/סכל** (SKL) Strong's #7919-20, 7922/ AHLB #2477

Ability to consider

Weigh information for gain

Understanding

Sense

Prudence

And when the woman saw that the tree *was* good for food, and that it *was* pleasant to the eyes, and a tree to be desired **to make one wise**, she took of the fruit thereof, and did eat, and gave also unto her husband with her; and he did eat.

וַתֵּרֶא הָאִשָּׁה כִּי טוֹב הָעֵץ
לְמַאֲכָל וְכִי תַאֲוָה־הוּא לָעֵינַיִם

וְנֶחְמָד הָעֵץ **לְהַשְׂכִּיל**
וַתִּקַּח מִפִּרְיוֹ וַתֹּאכַל וַתִּתֵּן גַּם־
לְאִישָׁהּ עִמָּהּ וַיֹּאכַל

Genesis 3:6

<u>שפט</u> (ShPTh) Strong's #4941,8196,8199,8200/ AHLB #2864

Judge

Created order and harmony

Regulate

Making decisions

The fear of Yahuah *is* clean, enduring for ever:
the **judgments** of Yahuah *are* true *and* righteous
altogether.

יִרְאַת יְהֹוָה ׀ טְהוֹרָה עוֹמֶדֶת
לָעַד **מִשְׁפְּטֵי**־יְהוָה אֱמֶת צָדְקוּ
יַחְדָּו

Psalm 19:9

## STUDY TWENTY-THREE

# Love: Ahav (אהב)

*So ought men to love their wives as their own bodies. He that loveth his wife loveth himself.*

**Ephesians 5:28**

אהב (AHB) Strong's #157,160,1890/ AHLB #1094

Love

Devoted completely to another

Relating intimately

Providing for the house

Conforming or being agreeable

Stimulate desire

Privileged gifts or burden


*And Isaac brought her into his mother Sarah's tent, and took Rebekah, and she became his wife; and he **loved** her: and Isaac was comforted after his mother's death.*

וַיְבִאֶהָ יִצְחָק הָאֹהֱלָה שָׂרָה אִמּוֹ
וַיִּקַּח אֶת־רִבְקָה וַתְּהִי־לוֹ לְאִשָּׁה
**וַיֶּאֱהָבֶהָ** וַיִּנָּחֵם יִצְחָק אַחֲרֵי אִמּוֹ

Genesis 24:67

# ⊙Ⴑь◻

<u>עגב</u> (AhGB) Strong's #5689,5691,5748/ AHLB #2523

Flirt

Sensuous tones

Lustfulness

Flute (piped instrument)

*And when thou art spoiled, what wilt thou do? Though thou clothest thyself with crimson, though thou deckest thee with ornaments of gold, though thou rentest thy face with painting, in vain shalt thou make thyself fair; **thy lovers** will despise thee, they will seek thy life.*

וְאַתִּי כ] (וְאַתְּ ק) שָׁדוּד מַה־
תַּעֲשִׂי כִּי־תִלְבְּשִׁי שָׁנִי כִּי־תַעְדִּי עֲדִי־
זָהָב כִּי־תִקְרְעִי בַפּוּךְ עֵינַיִךְ לַשָּׁוְא
תִּתְיַפִּי מָאֲסוּ־בָךְ **עֹגְבִים** נַפְשֵׁךְ
יְבַקֵּשׁוּ

Jeremiah 4:30

# אֱ‎חחם

**הבב** (HhB) Strong's #2243,2245/ AHLB #116

Hide

Bosom

Refuge

Wall of the house

Cherish

Passion

Protecting

Satisfaction

Love dutifully

Yea, he **loved** the people; all his saints *are* in thy hand: and they sat down at thy feet; *every one* shall receive of thy words.

אַף **חֹבֵב** עַמִּים כָּל־קְדֹשָׁיו בְּיָדֶךָ
וְהֵם תֻּכּוּ לְרַגְלֶךָ יִשָּׂא מִדַּבְּרֹתֶיךָ

Deuteronomy 33:3

# דד

**דד** (DWD) Strong's #1730-1,1733/ AHLB #1073

Support

Service needs

Friend

Beloved

Joyous love

Breasts

Boiling passion

Let him kiss me with the kisses of his mouth: for thy **love** *is* better than wine.

יִשָּׁקֵ֙נִי֙ מִנְּשִׁיק֣וֹת פִּ֔יהוּ כִּי־
טוֹבִ֥ים **דֹּדֶ֖יךָ** מִיָּֽיִן

Song of Solomon 1:2

### ⊶LLℲℲℲℲ

חשק (HhShQ) Strong's #2836-8/ AHLB #2219

Desire to hold close

Hugging

Encircling

Affection

Connection

Attached

Yahuah did not set his **love** upon you, nor choose you, because ye were more in number than any people; for ye *were* the fewest of all people:

לֹא מֵרֻבְּכֶם מִכָּל־הָעַמִּים **חָשַׁק**
יְהוָה בָּכֶם וַיִּבְחַר בָּכֶם כִּי־אַתֶּם הַמְעַט
מִכָּל־
הָעַמִּים

Deuteronomy 7:7

**רחם** (RHhM) Strong's #7356-60/ AHLB #2762

Protect from harm

Empathizing

Mercy

Tender love

Pity

And Elohim Almighty give you **mercy** before
the man, that he may send away your other
brother, and Benjamin. If I be bereaved *of my
children*, I am bereaved.

וְאֵל שַׁדַּי יִתֵּן לָכֶם **רַחֲמִים**
לִפְנֵי הָאִישׁ וְשִׁלַּח לָכֶם אֶת־
אֲחִיכֶם אַחֵר וְאֶת־בִּנְיָמִין וַאֲנִי
כַּאֲשֶׁר שָׁכֹלְתִּי שָׁכָלְתִּי

Genesis 43:14

**רעה** (RAhH) Strong's #7453, 7462-4,7470/ AHLB #1453

Tend

Satisfy

Spiritual sustenance

Unified

Shepherd

Growing

Knowing thoughts

Concerned

Man watches

Thou knowest my downsitting and mine upris-
ing, thou **<u>understandest</u>** my thought afar off.

אַתָּה יָדַעְתָּ שִׁבְתִּי וְקוּמִי בַּנְתָה
**לְרֵעִי** מֵרָחוֹק

Psalm 139:2

STUDY TWENTY-FOUR

# Chastise: Yasar (יסר)

He that spareth his rod hateth his son: but he that loveth him chasteneth him betimes.

**Proverbs 13:24**

<u>יסר</u> (Y-SR) Strong's #631,3256,4148/ AHLB #1342

To correct

To make a change in direction through correction

Turning head of a child or student

Punish

Instruct

Set limits/restrain

*And if ye will not be **reformed** by me by these things, but will walk contrary unto me; Then will I also walk contrary unto you, and will punish you yet seven times for your sins.*

וְאִם־בְּאֵלֶּה לֹא **תִוָּסְרוּ** לִי
וַהֲלַכְתֶּם עִמִּי קֶרִי וְהָלַכְתִּי אַף־

אֲנִי עִמָּכֶם בְּקֶרִי וְהִכֵּיתִי אֶתְכֶם
גַּם־אָנִי שֶׁבַע עַל־חַטֹּאתֵיכֶם

Leviticus 26:23-24

# ⴼⴼⵣⵉⵎ

י**כח** (YKHh) Strong's #3198 AHLB #1238

Chastise

Correct with a firm hand

Reprove

Rebuke

Plead/reason

Admonish

*For whom Yahuah loveth he **correcteth**; even as a father the son in whom he delighteth.*

כִּי אֶת אֲשֶׁר יֶאֱהַב יְהוָה **יוֹכִיחַ**
וּכְאָב אֶת־בֵּן יִרְצֶה

Proverbs 3:12

כ**שר** (KShR) Strong's #3787-8/ AHLB #2294

Prepare

Connect Properly

Being Skillful
Bonding
Act Right
In Line
Prosperity
Success

*Elohim setteth the solitary in families: he bringeth out those which are **bound** with chains: but the rebellious dwell in a dry land.*

אֱלֹהִים ׀ מוֹשִׁיב יְחִידִים ׀
בַּיְתָה מוֹצִיא אֲסִירִים **בַּכּוֹשָׁרוֹת**
אַךְ סוֹרֲרִים שָׁכְנוּ צְחִיחָה

Proverbs 68:6

כחח (KHHk) Strong's #3581,8433/ AHLB #1238

Exert power
Be strong
Right hand

*And in very deed for this cause have I raised thee up, for to shew in thee my **power**; and that my name may be declared throughout all the earth.*

וְאוּלָם בַּעֲבוּר זֹאת הֶעֱמַדְתִּיךָ
בַּעֲבוּר הַרְאֹתְךָ אֶת־**כֹּחִי** וּלְמַעַן סַפֵּר
שְׁמִי בְּכָל־
הָאָרֶץ.

Exodus 9:16

# ⌐⌐◉⌐⌐

**יגע** (Y-GAh) Strong's #3021-3/ AHLB #1062

Tire
Worn out
Weary
Exert one's self
labor

*And I will come upon him while he is **weary** and
weak handed, and will make him afraid: and all
the people that are with him shall flee; and I will
smite the king only:*

וְאָבוֹא עָלָיו וְהוּא **יָגֵעַ** וּרְפֵה
יָדַיִם וְהַחֲרַדְתִּי אֹתוֹ וְנָס כָּל־הָעָם
אֲשֶׁר־אִתּוֹ וְהִכֵּיתִי אֶת־הַמֶּלֶךְ
לְבַדּוֹ

2 Samuel 17:2

# 𐤋𐤁𐤄𐤔

**יגה** (YGH) Strong's #3013-4/ AHLB #1210

Suffer

Sorrow

removing

*The ways of Zion do mourn, because none come to the solemn feasts: all her gates are desolate: her priests sigh, her virgins are **afflicted**, and she is in bitterness.*

דַּרְכֵי צִיּוֹן אֲבֵלוֹת מִבְּלִי בָּאֵי מוֹעֵד
כָּל־שְׁעָרֶיהָ שׁוֹמֵמִין כֹּהֲנֶיהָ נֶאֱנָחִים
בְּתוּלֹתֶיהָ **נּוּגוֹת** וְהִיא מַר־לָהּ

Lamentations 1:4

# 𐤋𐤔𐤓

**ישר** (YShR) Strong's #3474/ AHLB #1480

Straighten

Faithful to duty

Tightly secure

Navel cord

Loosen cord

*Therefore I **<u>esteem</u>** all thy precepts concerning all things to be right; and I hate every false way.*

עַל־כֵּן ׀ כָּל־פִּקּוּדֵי כֹל יִשָּׁרְתִּי כָּל־אֹרַח שֶׁקֶר שָׂנֵאתִי

Psalm 119:128

---

# Wisdom: Chakam (חכם)

**חכם** (HhKM) Strong's #2449-52,2454 AHLB #2159

Accumulate knowledge

Absorb knowledge

Be wise

Learn

*The fear of Yahuah is the beginning of **wisdom**: and the knowledge of the holy is understanding.*

תְּחִלַּת **חָכְמָה** יִרְאַת יְהֹוֶה וְדַעַת קְדֹשִׁים בִּינָה

Proverbs 9:10

**בִין** (BYN) Strong's #995-9,1143/ AHLB #1037

Exert power

Be strong
Right hand

*Also Jonathan David's uncle was a counseller, a* **wise** *man, and a scribe: and Jehiel the son of Hachmoni was with the king's sons:*

וִיהוֹנָתָן דּוֹד־דָּוִיד יוֹעֵץ אִישׁ־**מֵבִין**
וְסוֹפֵר הוּא וִיחִיאֵל בֶּן־חַכְמוֹנִי עִם
־בְּנֵי הַמֶּלֶךְ

1 Chronicles 27:32

**טעם** (Th-AhM) Strong's #2938,2940/ AHLB #2236

Reason
Perceive
Sensing
Tasting
Distinguishing thoughts
Advice

*And blessed be thy* **advice**, *and blessed be thou, which hast kept me this day from coming to shed blood, and from avenging myself with mine own hand.*

וּבָרוּךְ **טַעְמֵךְ** וּבְרוּכָה אָתְּ
אֲשֶׁר כְּלִתִּנִי הַיּוֹם הַזֶּה מִבּוֹא
בְדָמִים וְהֹשֵׁעַ יָדִי לִי

1 Samuel 25:33

𐤎𐤔𐤋 / 𐤎𐤔𐤋

<u>סכל/שכל</u> (SKL) Strong's #7919/ AHLB #2477

Consider

Wisdom

Understand

Prosper

Success

*I will behave myself **wisely** in a perfect way. O when will you come unto me? I will walk within my house with a perfect heart.*

אַשְׂכִּילָה ׀ בְּדֶרֶךְ תָּמִים מָתַי
תָּבוֹא אֵלָי אֶתְהַלֵּךְ בְּתָם־לְבָבִי
בְּקֶרֶב בֵּיתִי

Psalm 101:2

# Order: Arak (ערך)

עֶרֶך (AhRK) Strong's #4634,6186-7/ AHLB #2576
Arrange side by side
Being an equal
Plan
Preparation
Furnish

*But she had brought them up to the roof of the house, and hid them with the stalks of flax, which she had **laid in order** upon the roof*

וְהִיא הֶעֱלָתַם הַגָּגָה וַתִּטְמְנֵם֙ בְּפִשְׁתֵּי הָעֵץ **הָעֲרֻכוֹת** לָהּ עַל־הַגָּג

Joshua 2:6

<u>כּין</u> (KWN) Strong's #3559,3561 AHLB #1244

Firm

Foundation

Guide

Fixed by words

**<u>Order</u>** my steps in thy word: and let not any iniquity have dominion over me.

פְּעָמַי **הָכֵן** בְּאִמְרָתֶךָ וְאַל־
תַּשְׁלֶט־בִּי כָל־אָוֶן

Psalm 119:133

<u>דבר</u> (D-BR) Strong's #1696/ AHLB #2093

The order in which something is performed

Arrangement

Bees (observationally)

Regulation

Collecting

Gathering

Subdue

Speak a command

*Then Judah came near unto him, and said, Oh my lord, let thy servant, I pray thee, speak a **word** in my lord's ears, and let not thine anger burn against thy servant: for thou art even as Pharaoh.*

וַיִּגַּשׁ אֵלָיו יְהוּדָה וַיֹּאמֶר בִּי
אֲדֹנִי יְדַבֶּר־נָא עַבְדְּךָ **דָבָר** בְּאָזְנֵי
אֲדֹנִי
וְאַל־יִחַר אַפְּךָ בְּעַבְדֶּךָ כִּי
כָמוֹךָ כְּפַרְעֹה

Genesis 44:18

𐤑𐤅𐤉𐤀𐤏

צוה (TsWH) Strong's #4687,6680/ AHLB #1397

Command
Appoint
Charge
Delegate authority

*Because that Abraham obeyed my voice, and kept my charge, my **commandments**, my statutes, and my laws.*

עֵקֶב אֲשֶׁר־שָׁמַע אַבְרָהָם בְּקֹלִי
וַיִּשְׁמֹר מִשְׁמַרְתִּי **מִצְוֺתַי** חֻקּוֹתַי
הָאָרֶץ.וְתוֹרֹתָי

Genesis 26:5

<u>סדר</u> (SDR) Strong's #5468, 7713/ AHLB #2468

Arrange

Set in order

Establish law

A row of planks when constructing a house

An army

*A land of darkness, as darkness itself; and of the shadow of death, without any **order**, and where the light is as darkness.*

אֶרֶץ עֵיפָתָה ׀ כְּמוֹ אֹפֶל
צַלְמָוֶת וְלֹא **סְדָרִים** וַתֹּפַע כְּמוֹ־
אֹפֶל

Job 10:22

# פ/ש/פ

שלב (ShLB) Strong's #7947-8/ AHLB 2840

Step

Level

Bound

Joined

Equal order

*Two tenons shall there be in one board, **set in order** one against another: thus shalt thou make for all the boards of the tabernacle.*

שְׁתֵּי יָדֹות לַקֶּרֶשׁ הָאֶחָד
**מְשֻׁלָּבֹת** אִשָּׁה אֶל־אֲחֹתָהּ כֵּן
תַּעֲשֶׂה לְכֹל קַרְשֵׁי הַמִּשְׁכָּן

Exodus 26:17

תקן (TQN) Strong's #3474/ AHLB #1480

Ready

Complete

Straightening

Participating

Be made straight

Put in place
Proper alignment

*That which is crooked cannot **be made straight**:*
*and that which is wanting cannot be numbered...*

וְחֶסְרוֹן **לְתַקֵּן** לֹא־יוּכַל מְעֻוָּת
לְהִמָּנוֹת לֹא־יוּכָל

Ecclesiastes 1:15

STUDY TWENTY-SEVEN

# Teach: Yarah (ירה)

ꓕꓭꓷ⅃

**ירה** (Y-RH) Strong's #3138,3384/ AHLB #1227

Cast

Shoot forth to a particular place

Early rain

Throwing of a hand to a direction to live or walk

Awe or fear of calamity

Point in the way of life

*That I will give you the rain of your land in his due season, **the first rain** and the latter rain, that thou mayest gather in thy corn, and thy wine, and thine oil.*

וְנָתַתִּי מְטַר־אַרְצְכֶם בְּעִתּוֹ

**יוֹרֶה** וּמַלְקוֹשׁ וְאָסַפְתָּ דְגָנֶךָ

וְתִירֹשְׁךָ וְיִצְהָרֶךָ

Deuteronomy 11:14

בִין (BNN) Strong's #995 AHLB #1244

Consider carefully

Diligently consider

Discern

Penetrate to the core

Thorough reasoning

Making known

*My son, attend unto my wisdom, and bow thine ear to **my understanding**:*

בְּנִי לְחָכְמָתִי הַקְשִׁיבָה **לִתְבוּנָתִי** הַט־אָזְנֶךָ

Proverbs 5:1

לִיץ (LYTS) Strong's #3887/ AHLB #1271

Interpret

Ambassador

Mediator

The authority of the tongue

Speaking a language and needing an interpreter

*And they knew not that Joseph under-*
*stood them; for he spake unto them by **an inter-***
***preter.***

וְהֵם֙ לֹ֣א יָֽדְע֔וּ כִּ֥י שֹׁמֵ֖עַ יוֹסֵ֑ף כִּ֥י
**הַמֵּלִ֖יץ** בֵּינֹתָֽם

Genesis 42:23

עדי

**יֽדע** (YDA) Strong's #3045/ AHLB #1085

To have an intimate relationship with a person, idea, or
experience
Be aware
Knowledge
Recognizing
Door of the eye

*For Elohim doth know that in the day ye eat*
*thereof, then your eyes shall be opened, and ye*
*shall be as gods, **knowing** good and evil.*

כִּ֚י יֹדֵ֣עַ אֱלֹהִ֔ים כִּ֗י בְּיוֹם֙
אֲכָלְכֶ֣ם מִמֶּ֔נּוּ וְנִפְקְח֖וּ עֵֽינֵיכֶ֑ם
וִהְיִיתֶם֙ כֵּֽאלֹהִ֔ים **יֹדְעֵ֖י** ט֥וֹב וָרָֽע

Genesis 3:5

<u>אלף</u> (ALPh) Strong's #502/ AHLB #2001

Guide, yoke, learn
To learn by example
To bring forth 100 fold
Younger taught by the more experienced
Husband
Friend

*If not, hearken unto me: hold thy peace, and I shall **teach** thee wisdom.*

אִם־אַיִן אַתָּה שְׁמַע־לִי הַחֲרֵשׁ
**וַאֲאַלֶּפְךָ** חָכְמָה

Job 33:33

<u>זהר</u> (ZHR) Strong's #2094-5/ AHLB #1158

Warn of limits
Admonish
Shine light in a direction or onto something
Heed

*Moreover by them is thy servant* **warned**: *and in keeping of them there is great reward.*

גַּם־עַבְדְּךָ **נִזְהָר** בָּהֶם בְּשָׁמְרָם עֵקֶב רָב

Psalm 19:11

שׁנן (ShNN) Strong's #8150/ AHLB #1474

Sharpen

Focus

Teaching repeatedly

Tearing apart and digesting

Precision

Direct speech

**And thou shalt teach them** *diligently unto thy children, and shalt talk of them when thou sittest in thine house, and when thou walkest by the way, and when thou liest down, and when thou risest up.*

**וְשִׁנַּנְתָּם** לְבָנֶיךָ וְדִבַּרְתָּ בָּם בְּשִׁבְתְּךָ בְּבֵיתֶךָ וּבְלֶכְתְּךָ בַדֶּרֶךְ וּבְשָׁכְבְּךָ וּבְקוּמֶךָ

Deuteronomy 6:7

# ꟻ ᴟ𐤃

## לָמַד (LMD) Strong's #3925,3928,4451/ AHLB 2311

Learn

Learn by chastisement or goading

Instruct

Expert

Skillful

Directing oxen in yoke

Learn from behavior

Habituating

Disciple/ Student

*Now therefore hearken, O Israel, unto the statutes and unto the judgments, which I **teach** you, for to do them, that ye may live, and go in and possess the land which Yahuah Elohim of your fathers giveth you.*

וְעַתָּה יִשְׂרָאֵל שְׁמַע אֶל־הַחֻקִּים וְאֶל־
הַמִּשְׁפָּטִים אֲשֶׁר אָנֹכִי **מְלַמֵּד** אֶתְכֶם
לַעֲשׂוֹת לְמַעַן תִּחְיוּ וּבָאתֶם וִירִשְׁתֶּם
אֶת־הָאָרֶץ אֲשֶׁר יְהוָה אֱלֹהֵי אֲבֹתֵיכֶם
נֹתֵן לָכֶם׃

Deuteronomy 4:1

# ᒍᄂᎻᎱᒍ

**שכל** (SKL) Strong's #7919,7920,7922/ AHLB #2477

Understand

Adapt to needs

Causing to succeed

Absorb information

Instructing for comprehension

Knowingly guiding

Acting rationally

*O that they were wise, that they* **understood**
*this, that they would consider their latter end!*

אִלוּ חָכְמוּ יַשְׂכִּילוּ זֹאת יָבִינוּ
לְאַחֲרִיתָם

Deuteronomy 32:29

## STUDY TWENTY-EIGHT

---

# "Weaker" Vessel: Keli (כלי)

*Likewise, ye husbands, dwell with them according to knowledge, giving honour unto the wife, as unto the weaker vessel, and as being heirs together of the grace of life; that your prayers be not hindered.*
**1 Peter 3:7**

# עש/ךּ

כלה (K-LH) Strong's #3618 / AHLB #1242

Strive to attain

Yearn

Organ of Yearning

Bride

Consummation

Complete/whole

Tame for the yoke

*Thou has ravished my heart, my sister, my **spouse**; thou hast ravished my heart with one of thine eyes, with one chain of thy neck.*

לִבַּבְתִּנִי אֲחֹתִי **כַלָּה**
לִבַּבְתִּנִי [בְּאַחַד כ] (בְּאַחַת ק)
מֵעֵינַיִךְ בְּאַחַד
עֲנָק מִצַּוְּרֹנָיִךְ

Song of Solomon 4:9

<u>תאנה</u> (TA-NH) Strong's #579,8385 AHLB #1014

Produce
Sending for one to have an encounter
Opportunity
Donkey (wild ass)


*A wild ass used to the wilderness, that snuffeth
up the wind at her pleasure; in her occasion
who can turn her away? all they that seek her
will not weary themselves; in her month they
shall find her.*


פֶּרֶה ׀ לִמֻּד מִדְבָּר בְּאַוַּת [נַפְשׁוֹ כ]
(נַפְשָׁהּ ק) שָׁאֲפָה רוּחַ **תַּאֲנָתָהּ** מִי
יְשִׁיבֶנָּה כָּל־מְבַקְשֶׁיהָ לֹא יִיעָפוּ
בְּחָדְשָׁהּ יִמְצָאוּנְהָ

Jeremiah 2:24

נבל (NBL) Strong's #5035/ AHLB #1035,2639

Interpret

Ambassador

Mediator

The authority of the tongue

Speaking a language and needing an interpreter

*And he shall break it as the breaking of the potters' **vessel** that is broken in pieces; he shall not spare: so that there shall not be found in the bursting of it a sherd to take fire from the hearth, or to take water withal out of the pit.*

וּשְׁבָרָהּ כְּשֵׁבֶר **נֵבֶל** יוֹצְרִים כָּתוּת
לֹא יַחְמֹל וְלֹא־יִמָּצֵא בִמְכִתָּתוֹ חֶרֶשׂ
לַחְתּוֹת אֵשׁ מִיָּקוּד וְלַחְשֹׂף מַיִם
מִגֶּבֶא

Isaiah 30:14

STUDY TWENTY-NINE

# Beautiful: Yapheh (יפה)

*Thou art all fair, my love; there is no spot in thee.*
**Song of Solomon 4:7**

<u>יפה</u> (YPH) Strong's #3302-3/ AHLB #1224

Goes beyond the normal

A wonder

Excite the senses

*And it came to pass, when he was come near to enter into Egypt, that he said unto Sarai his wife, Behold now, I know that thou art a* **fair** *woman to look upon:*

וַיְהִי כַּאֲשֶׁר הִקְרִיב לָבוֹא
מִצְרָיְמָה וַיֹּאמֶר אֶל־שָׂרַי אִשְׁתּוֹ
הִנֵּה־נָא יָדַעְתִּי כִּי אִשָּׁה **יְפַת**־
מַרְאֶה אָתְּ

Genesis 12:11

# ⊗ⴌY⊓

**טוב** (THWB) Strong's #2876,2895,2898 AHLB #1186

Advance benefit to man

Good and pleasant

Functional

Happy

Healthy

Treat well

Surround the house

Being purposeful

Being beautful

*And he said, I will make all my **goodness** pass before thee, and I will proclaim the name of Ya-huah before thee; and will be gracious to whom I will be gracious, and will shew mercy on whom I will shew mercy.*

וַיֹּ֗אמֶר אֲנִ֨י אַעֲבִ֤יר כָּל־**טוּבִי֙** עַל־
פָּנֶ֔יךָ וְקָרָ֧אתִי בְשֵׁ֛ם יְהֹוָ֖ה לְפָנֶ֑יךָ
וְחַנֹּתִי֙ אֶת־אֲשֶׁ֣ר אָחֹ֔ן וְרִחַמְתִּ֖י
אֶת־אֲשֶׁ֥ר אֲרַחֵֽם

Exodus 33:19

**יפע** (YPAh) Strong's #3313/ AHLB #1384

Radiate

Emerge from darkness

Brightness awaken

Send out beams

*Out of Zion, the perfection of **beauty**, Elohim hath shined.*

מִצִּיּוֹן מִכְלַל-**יֹפִי** אֱלֹהִים הוֹפִיעַ

Psalm 50:2

**נאה** (N-AH) Strong's #4998,5000/ AHLB #130

Pleasant

Comely

Appropriate

Lovely

Pleasant habitation

comfort

*Rejoice in Yahuah, O ye righteous: for praise is **comely** for the upright..*

רַנְּנוּ צַדִּיקִים בַּיהוָה לַיְשָׁרִים
**נָאוָה** תְהִלָּה

Psalm 33:1

<u>פרה</u> (P-RH) Strong's #6500,6509/ AHLB #1388

Fruitful

Increase

Reveal the seed

Decoration

Progeny

*Thy wife shall be as a **fruitful** vine by the sides of thine house: thy children like olive plants round about thy table.*

אֶשְׁתְּךָ ׀ כְּגֶפֶן **פֹּרִיָּה** בְּיַרְכְּתֵי
בֵיתֶךָ בָּנֶיךָ כִּשְׁתִלֵי זֵיתִים סָבִיב
לְשֻׁלְחָנֶךָ

Psalm 128:3

<u>עטר</u> (AhThR) Strong's #5849,5850/ AHLB #2538

Wreath

Sign of Authority
Wrapped
Encircle (Guarded)
Bounds of Territory
Distinguish

*She shall give to thine head an ornament of grace: a **crown** of glory shall she deliver to thee.*

תִּתֵּן לְרֹאשְׁךָ לִוְיַת־חֵן
**עֲטֶרֶת** תִּפְאֶרֶת תְּמַגְּנֶךָּ

Proverbs 4:9

פאר (P-AR) Strong's #6289/ AHLB #1388

Distinguish
Standout
Distinctive
See in good light
Bravery
Blackness
Turban upon the head
Honor

*In that day the Lord will take away the **bravery** of their tinkling ornaments about their feet,*

*and their cauls, and their round tires like the*
*moon,*

בַּיּוֹם הַהוּא יָסִיר אֲדֹנָי אֵת **תִּפְאֶרֶת**
הָעֲכָסִים וְהַשְּׁבִיסִים וְהַשַּׂהֲרֹנִים

Isaiah 3:18

# Vanity: Ayn (אֵין)

*Beware lest any man spoil you through philosophy and vain deceit, after the tradition of men, after the rudiments of the world, and not after Christ.*
**Colossians 2:8**

אֵין (AYN) Strong's #369 AHLB #1014

Vanity

Absent of

Using the power of the lower region

Creative work for empty purposes

Mischief

Unable to do or have something

Work with no results

*But Sarai was barren; she had* **no** *child.*

וַתְּהִי שָׂרַי עֲקָרָה **אֵין** לָהּ וָלָד
Genesis 11:30

ריק (RYQ) Strong's #7385-6/ AHLB #1456
Empty of all contents
Take away from nutrients

*I also will do this unto you; I will even appoint over you terror, consumption, and the burning ague, that shall consume the eyes, and cause sorrow of heart: and ye shall sow your seed __in vain__, for your enemies shall eat it.*

אַף־אֲנִ֞י אֶעֱשֶׂה־זֹּ֣את לָכֶ֗ם
וְהִפְקַדְתִּ֨י עֲלֵיכֶ֤ם בֶּֽהָלָה֙ אֶת־
הַשַּׁחֶ֣פֶת וְאֶת־הַקַּדַּ֔חַת מְכַלּ֥וֹת
עֵינַ֖יִם וּמְדִיבֹ֣ת נָ֑פֶשׁ וּזְרַעְתֶּ֤ם
__לָרִיק֙__ זַרְעֲכֶ֔ם וַאֲכָלֻ֖הוּ אֹיְבֵיכֶֽם

Leviticus 26:16

� symbol

והו (THW) Strong's #8414,8429/ AHLB #1488
A barren place
To consider of no value
Empty space

Waste place

*None calleth for justice, nor any pleadeth for truth: they trust in **vanity**, and speak lies; they conceive mischief, and bring forth iniquity.*

אֵין־קֹרֵא בְצֶדֶק וְאֵין נִשְׁפָּט
בֶּאֱמוּנָה בָּטוֹחַ עַל־**תֹּהוּ** וְדַבֶּר־שָׁוְא
הָרוֹ עָמָל וְהוֹלֵיד אָוֶן

Isaiah 59:4

הבל (HBL) Strong's #1892/ AHLB #1035

Vapor
Lack value
Breath
Temporary

*They have moved me to jealousy with that which is not Elohim; they have provoked me to anger with their **vanities**[1]: and I will move them to jealousy with those which are not a people; I will provoke them to anger with a foolish nation.*

---

[1] This word is also translated as idol in other versions of scripture.

הֵם קִנְאוּנִי בְלֹא־אֵל כִּעֲסוּנִי
**בְּהַבְלֵיהֶם** וַאֲנִי אַקְנִיאֵם בְּלֹא־
עָם בְּגוֹי נָבָל אַכְעִיסֵם

Deuteronomy 32:21

# ש�𐤀�


שׁוֹא (ShWA) Strong's #7723/ AHLB #1461

Desolate

Destroy

Leave Empty


*Thou shalt not take the name of Yahuah thy Elohim in vain; for Yahuah will not hold him guiltless that taketh his name in vain.*

לֹא תִשָּׂא אֶת־שֵׁם־יְהֹוָה אֱלֹהֶיךָ
לַשָּׁוְא כִּי לֹא יְנַקֶּה יְהֹוָה אֵת אֲשֶׁר־
יִשָּׂא אֶת־שְׁמוֹ
לַשָּׁוְא

Exodus 20:7

## STUDY THIRTY-ONE

# Hair: Sear (שער)

*His head and his hairs were white like wool, as white as snow; and his eyes were as a flame of fire;*
**Revelation 1:14**

שער\ס (HBL) Strong's #1892/ AHLB #1035

Fearing/ dreading

Growing hair

Shine

Illuminate

Encircle

Storm cloud

*And when he polled his head, (for it was at every year's end that he polled it: because the hair was heavy on him, therefore he polled it:) he weighed the **hair** of his head at two hundred shekels after the king's weight.*

וּבְגַלְּחוֹ אֶת־רֹאשׁוֹ וְהָיָה מִקֵּץ
יָמִים ׀ לַיָּמִים אֲשֶׁר יְגַלֵּחַ כִּי־כָבֵד
עָלָיו וְגִלְּחוֹ וְשָׁקַל אֶת־**שְׂעַר**
רֹאשׁוֹ מָאתַיִם שְׁקָלִים בְּאֶבֶן
הַמֶּלֶךְ

2 Samuel 14:26

# 𐤱𐤋𐤪

דלה (DLH) Strong's #1802,1808-9 AHLB #1081

What hangs from the head

Blown in the wind

Drawing up water

High hanging branches

Raised hair (afro)

*Counsel in the heart of man is like deep water;*
*but a man of understanding **will draw it out**.*

מַיִם עֲמֻקִים עֵצָה בְלֶב־אִישׁ וְאִישׁ
תְּבוּנָה **יִדְלֶנָּה**²
Proverbs 20:5

# 𐤱𐤮�

קשה (QShH) Strong's #4748/ AHLB #1435

Bunched hair

Solid piece of hair

Ensnare

Covered

Gather

---

² This word gives us an interesting to the story of Samson and Delilah (same root word). She drew out the truth from Samson about his hair.

Stalk of grain with a cord wrapped around the middle

*And it shall come to pass, that instead of sweet smell there shall be stink; and instead of a girdle a rent; and instead of **well set hair** baldness; and instead of a stomacher a girding of sackcloth; and burning instead of beauty.*

וְהָיָה֩ תַ֨חַת בֹּ֜שֶׂם מַ֣ק יִֽהְיֶ֗ה
וְתַ֨חַת חֲגוֹרָ֤ה נִקְפָּה֙ וְתַ֤חַת מַֽעֲשֶׂה֙
**מִקְשֶׁה֙** קׇרְחָ֔ה וְתַ֖חַת פְּתִיגִ֑יל
מַחֲגֹ֣רֶת שָׂ֑ק כִּי־תַ֖חַת יֹֽפִי

Isaiah 3:24

**נזר** (N-ZR) Strong's #5139,5144-5/ AHLB #2390
Crown
Separation
Unattended vine
Nazarite
Dedicate
Shaved head of dedication

*The blessings of thy father have prevailed above the blessings of my progenitors unto the utmost* *bound of the everlasting hills: they shall be on the head of Joseph, and on the crown of the head of him that was **separate** ³from his brethren.*

בִּרְכֹת אָבִיךָ גָּבְרוּ עַל־בִּרְכֹת הוֹרַי עַד־תַּאֲוַת גִּבְעֹת עוֹלָם תִּהְיֶיןָ לְרֹאשׁ יוֹסֵף וּלְקָדְקֹד **נְזִיר** אֶחָיו

Genesis 49:26

<u>פרע</u> (PRA) Strong's #6545/ AHLB #2641

Long
Lose of cut hair
Lose complete control
Wild hair
locks

*And the priest shall set the woman before Yahuah, **and uncover**⁴ the woman's head, and put the offering of memorial in her hands, which is the jealousy offering: and the priest shall*

---

³ It is possible that Joseph was set apart as a Nazarite.
⁴ To cut her hair

*have in his hand the bitter water that causeth the curse*

וְהֶעֱמִ֨יד הַכֹּהֵ֥ן אֶת־הָֽאִשָּׁה֮ לִפְנֵ֣י יְהוָה֒ **וּפָרַע֙** אֶת־רֹ֣אשׁ הָֽאִשָּׁ֔ה וְנָתַ֣ן עַל־כַּפֶּ֗יהָ אֵ֚ת מִנְחַ֣ת הַזִּכָּרֹ֔ון מִנְחַ֥ת קְנָאֹ֖ת הִ֑וא וּבְיַ֣ד הַכֹּהֵ֗ן יִהְי֛וּ מֵ֥י הַמָּרִ֖ים הַֽמְאָֽרֲרִֽים

Numbers 5:18

---

# Heart/Soul: Leb (לב)

## שׁפ‎ל

לב‎ (LBB) Strong's #3820,3823-5/ AHLB #1255

Joined at the core

Conquering the heart

Inner man

Mind

Understanding

Ego

*Then Abraham fell upon his face, and laughed, and said **in his heart**, Shall a child be born unto him that is an hundred years old? and shall Sarah, that is ninety years old, bear?*

וַיִּפֹּ֧ל אַבְרָהָ֛ם עַל־פָּנָ֖יו וַיִּצְחָ֑ק
וַיֹּ֣אמֶר **בְּלִבּ֗וֹ** הַלְּבֶ֤ן מֵאָֽה־שָׁנָה֙ יִוָּלֵ֔ד
וְאִם־שָׂרָ֔ה הֲבַת־תִּשְׁעִ֥ים שָׁנָ֖ה תֵּלֵֽד

Genesis 17:17

**נפש** (NPhSh) Strong's #5315/ AHLB #2523

Soul giving life to the body

Determination

Living personality

What makes a person an individual

Passion

Emotion

Desire

*But he himself went a day's journey into the wilderness, and came and sat down under a juniper tree: and he requested for himself that he might die; and said, It is enough; now, O LORD, take away **my life**; for I am not better than my fathers.*

וְהוּא־הָלַךְ בַּמִּדְבָּר דֶּרֶךְ יוֹם
וַיָּבֹא וַיֵּשֶׁב תַּחַת רֹתֶם [אַחַת כ]
(אֶחָד ק) וַיִּשְׁאַל אֶת־נַפְשׁוֹ לָמוּת
וַיֹּאמֶר ׀ רַב עַתָּה יְהוָה קַח **נַפְשִׁי**
כִּי־לֹא־טוֹב אָנֹכִי מֵאֲבֹתָי

1 Kings 19:4

STUDY THIRTY-THREE

---

# Witchcraft or Inquiring: Owb (אוב)

*For rebellion is as the sin of witchcraft, and stubbornness is as iniquity and idolatry.*
**1 Samuel 15:23**

## אוב (AWB) Strong's #178/ AHLB #1002

Oracle invoking rain

Necromancer

Mediums

Carrying a false ones name (making someone your father)

Hallowed vessel

Allowing spirits to speak through you

Ventriloquist

*Regard not them **that have familiar spirits**, neither seek after wizards, to be defiled by them: I am Yahuah your Elohim.*

אַל־תִּפְנוּ אֶל־**הָאֹבת** וְאֶל־הַיִּדְּעֹנִים אַל־
תְּבַקְשׁוּ לְטָמְאָה בָהֶם אֲנִי יְהוָה אֱלֹהֵיכֶם
Leviticus 19:31

## דרש (DRSh) Strong's #1875,4097/ AHLB #2114

Seeking

Inquiring

Demanding return of something (an answer)

Studying expounding

Investigating

Worship a deity

*And the children struggled together within her; and she said, If it be so, why am I thus? And she went to **inquire** of Yahuah.*

וַיִּתְרֹצֲצוּ הַבָּנִים בְּקִרְבָּהּ וַתֹּאמֶר אִם־כֵּן לָמָּה זֶּה אָנֹכִי וַתֵּלֶךְ **לִדְרֹשׁ** אֶת־יְהוָה

Genesis 25:22

## שאל (S-AL) Strong's #7592-3/ AHLB #1472

Request movement

Demand removal

Grave demanding the return of the body

Asking

Seeking what is unknown
Desire
Draw out

*Is it not wheat harvest to day? I will call unto Yahuah, and he shall send thunder and rain; that ye may perceive and see that your wickedness is great, which ye have done in the sight of Yahuah, **in asking** you a king.*

הֲלֹוא קְצִיר־חִטִּים הַיֹּום אֶקְרָא
אֶל־יְהֹוָה וְיִתֵּן קֹלֹות וּמָטָר וּדְעוּ
וּרְאוּ כִּי־רָעַתְכֶם רַבָּה אֲשֶׁר
עֲשִׂיתֶם בְּעֵינֵי יְהֹוָה **לִשְׁאֹול** לָכֶם
מֶלֶךְ

1 Samuel 12:17

J◌שׁ

<u>הבר</u> (HBL) Strong's #1895/ AHLB #1043
Analyze
Astrologers
Divide the stars
Eat, divide
Covenant through joint sacrifice
Join through communion

*Thou art wearied in the multitude of thy counsels. Let now the **astrologers**, the stargazers, the monthly prognosticators, stand up, and save thee from these things that shall come upon thee.*

נִלְאֵית בְּרֹב עֲצָתָיִךְ יַעַמְדוּ־נָא
וְיוֹשִׁיעֻךְ [**הָבְרוּ** כ] (**הֹבְרֵי** ק) שָׁמַיִם
הַחֹזִים בַּכּוֹכָבִים מוֹדִיעִם לֶחֳדָשִׁים
מֵאֲשֶׁר יָבֹאוּ עָלָיִךְ

Isaiah 47:13

<u>עָנָן</u> (ANN) Strong's #6050-1,6053/ AHLB #1359
Cloud
To watch
The eye
Watching over something of importance
To tell the weather/climate
Watch the clouds
 Looking to the sky

*There shall not be found among you any one that maketh his son or his daughter to pass through*

*the fire, or that useth divination, or **an observer
of times**, or an enchanter, or a witch*

לֹא־יִמָּצֵא בְךָ֖ מַעֲבִ֥יר בְּנֽוֹ־וּבִתּ֖וֹ
בָּאֵ֑שׁ קֹסֵ֣ם קְסָמִ֔ים **מְעוֹנֵ֥ן** וּמְנַחֵ֖שׁ
וּמְכַשֵּֽׁף

Deuteronomy 18:10

ᴧᴧ 𐤅‒o‒

קסם (QSM) Strong's #7080-1/ AHLB #2718

Divination
Perform feat beyond comprehension
Soothsayer

*And the elders of Moab and the elders of Midian
departed with the rewards of **divination** in their
hand; and they came unto Balaam, and spake
unto him the words of Balak.*

וַיֵּ֨לְכ֜וּ זִקְנֵ֤י מוֹאָב֙ וְזִקְנֵ֣י מִדְיָ֔ן
**וּקְסָמִ֖ים** בְּיָדָ֑ם וַיָּבֹ֙אוּ֙ אֶל־בִּלְעָ֔ם
וַיְדַבְּר֥וּ אֵלָ֖יו דִּבְרֵ֥י בָלָֽק

Numbers 22:7

**לחש** <u>(LKhSh) Strong's #3907-8/ AHLB #2308</u>

Whisper

Enchantment

Amulet to which prayers are directed

Surely the serpent will bite without **enchant-**
**ment**; and a babbler is no better.

אִם־יִשֹּׁךְ הַנָּחָשׁ בְּלוֹא־**לַחַשׁ** וְאֵין
יִתְרוֹן לְבַעַל הַלָּשׁוֹן

Ecclesiastes 10:11

**יִדְּעֹנִי** <u>(Ydani) Strong's #3049/ AHLB #1085</u>

One with special knowledge

Familiar spirit

*And he made his son pass through the fire, and*
*observed times, and used enchantments, and*
*dealt with **familiar spirits** and wizards: he*
*wrought much wickedness in the sight of Yahuah,*
*to provoke him to anger.*

וְהֶעֱבִיר אֶת־בְּנוֹ בָּאֵשׁ וְעוֹנֵן וְנִחֵשׁ
וְעָשָׂה אוֹב **וְיִדְּעֹנִים** הִרְבָּה לַעֲשׂוֹת
הָרַע בְּעֵינֵי
יְהוָה לְהַכְעִיס

2 Kings 21:6

# שחכ

כחש (KhHhSh) Strong's #3584-6/ AHLB #2257

Lying

Denying

Disappointing

Deceive

Fail

Withholding or denying something which causes lean-ness

Making weak or frail through a lie

Pretending

*And it shall come to pass in that day, that the prophets shall be ashamed every one of his vision, when he hath prophesied; neither shall they wear a rough garment to* **deceive**:

וְהָיָה ׀ בַּיּוֹם הַהוּא יֵבֹשׁוּ הַנְּבִיאֵים
אִישׁ מֵחֶזְיֹנוֹ בְּהִנָּבְאֹתוֹ וְלֹא יִלְבְּשׁוּ
אַדֶּרֶת שֵׂעָר לְמַעַן **כַּחֵשׁ**

Zechariah 13:4

STUDY THIRTY-FOUR

# Encourage: Chazaq (חזק)

*But ye, beloved, building up yourselves on your most holy faith, praying in the Holy Ghost,*

**Jude 1:20**

חזק (HhZQ) Strong's #2388,2392/ AHLB #2152

Hold tightly

strengthen

Being courageous

Pressing toward a goal

Fastening

Seize

Prepare for battle

*But Joshua the son of Nun, which standeth before thee, he shall go in thither: **encourage** him: for he shall cause Israel to inherit it.*

יְהוֹשֻׁעַ בִּן־נוּן הָעֹמֵד לְפָנֶיךָ הוּא יָבֹא
שָׁמָּה אֹתוֹ **חַזֵּק** כִּי־הוּא יַנְחִלֶנָּה אֶת־יִשְׂרָאֵל

Deuteronomy 1:38

---

# Vengeance: Naqam (נקם)

Dearly beloved, avenge not yourselves, but rather give place unto wrath: for
it is written, Vengeance is mine; I will repay, saith Yahuah.

**Romans 12:19**

נקם (HhZQ) Strong's #5358/ AHLB #1427,2433

Avenge

One who raises hand to another

To stand up against


*Thou shalt not **avenge,** nor bear any grudge
against the children of thy people, but thou shalt
love thy neighbour as thyself: I am Yahuah*

לֹא־**תִקֹּם** וְלֹא־תִטֹּר אֶת־בְּנֵי עַמֶּךָ
וְאָהַבְתָּ לְרֵעֲךָ כָּמוֹךָ אֲנִי יְהוָה

Leviticus 19:18

# Contentious: Madon (מדון)

**מדון** (MDN) Strong's #1777, 4066, 4079, 4090/ AHLB #1083

Sentencing
Final judgment
Defend
Dispute
Vindictive
Brawling
Rule over
Discord

It is better to dwell in a corner of the housetop, than with a brawling[5] women in a wide house.

טוֹב לָשֶׁבֶת עַל־פִּנַת־גָּג מֵאֵשֶׁת
**מִדְיָנִים** וּבֵית חָבֶר
Proverbs 21:9

---

[5] contentious

### STUDY THIRTY-SEVEN

# Foolish: Lo (לוא)

לוא (LO) Strong's #191,194,196,3808,3863/ AHLB #1254

Idol

To be without

Foolish

Without wisdom

For my people *is* foolish, they have not known me; they *are* sottish children, and they have none understanding: they *are* wise to do evil, but to do good they have no knowledge.

כִּי | **אֱוִיל**[6] עַמִּי אוֹתִי לֹא יָדָעוּ בָּנִים
סְכָלִים הֵמָּה וְלֹא נְבוֹנִים
הֵמָּה חֲכָמִים הֵמָּה לְהָרַע
וּלְהֵיטִיב **לֹא** יָדָעוּ

Jeremiah 4:22

---

[6] one of the words for foolish in Hebrew is evil **אויל**. Look up this word in your

### נבל (NBL) Strong's #1077,1097,1099,1101,5036,8399/ AHLB #2396

Flow

To come to nothing when effort is given

Exchange

Confusion (act lacking results)

Do ye thus requite Yahuah, O **foolish** people and unwise? *is* not he thy father *that* hath bought thee? hath he not made thee, and established thee?

$$\text{הֲ־לַיהוָה֙ תִּגְמְלוּ־זֹ֔את עַ֖ם נָבָ֣ל}$$
$$\text{וְלֹ֣א חָכָ֑ם הֲלוֹא־הוּא֙ אָבִ֣יךָ קָּנֶ֔ךָ ה֖וּא}$$
$$\text{עָֽשְׂךָ֖ וַֽיְכֹנְנֶֽךָ}$$

Deuteronomy 32:6

### כסל (CSL) Strong's #3684,3688,5528/ AHLB #2275

Loins

Confidence

Confidence in something foolish

Folly

Boasting in your loins

Understand, ye brutish among the people: and *ye* **fools**, when will ye be wise?

בִּינוּ בֹּעֲרִים בָּעָם **וּכְסִילִים** מָתַי תַּשְׂכִּילוּ

Psalm 94:8

⊙†↲

**פתי** (PTY) Strong's #6612/ AHLB #1390

Gullible

Seducing

Responding to outside influences

Place of debauchery

Full of wholes

A hole for intercourse

Inexperienced

The **simple** believeth every word: but the prudent *man* looketh well to his going.

**פֶּתִי** יַאֲמִין לְכָל־דָּבָר וְעָרוֹם יָבִין לַאֲשֻׁרוֹ

Proverbs 14:15

**בער** (BER) Strong's #1198/ AHLB #2028

Senseless

Brutish

Burn

Kindle fire

So **_foolish_** was I, and ignorant: I was as a beast before thee.

וַאֲנִי־**בַעַר** וְלֹא אֵדָע בְּהֵמוֹת הָיִיתִי עִמָּךְ

Psalm 73:22

**תפל** (TPL) Strong's #8602,8604 AHLB #2898

Tasteless

Untampered

Foolish

Folly

Worthless

*Thy prophets have seen vain and **<u>foolish</u>** things for thee: and they have not discovered thine iniquity, to turn away thy captivity; but have seen for thee false burdens and causes of banishment.*

נְבִיאַ֗יִךְ חָ֤זוּ לָךְ֙ שָׁ֣וְא **וְתָפֵ֔ל** וְלֹֽא־גִלּ֥וּ עַל־עֲוֺנֵ֖ךְ לְהָשִׁ֣יב [שְׁבִיתֵ֑ךְ כ] (שְׁבוּתֵ֑ךְ ק)
וַיֶּ֣חֱזוּ לָ֔ךְ מַשְׂא֥וֹת שָׁ֖וְא וּמַדּוּחִֽים

Lamentations 2:14

## STUDY THIRTY-EIGHT

# Bride/Wife: Kallah (כלה)

*An excellent wife is the crown of her husband, But she who shames him is like rottenness in his bones.*

**Proverbs 12:14**

# עשׁJJ

**כלל** (KLL) Strong's #3618,3623,3623,3634-5,4359/ AHLB #1242

The choice piece

Perfection

Vessel

Consummation

Tame for the yoke

A container for holding contents

Bride (one who makes man complete)

Out of Zion, the **perfection** of beauty, Elohim hath shined..

מִצִּיּוֹן **מִכְלַל**־יֹפִי אֱלֹהִים הוֹפִיעַ

Psalm 50:2

## בעל (BAL) Strong's #1166-7,1169/ AHLB #2027

Dominion

Owning

Rule

Marrying

Having a husband

Head of

Wooing

Mastering

Possession

Idolatry

Bind/yoke

*Thou shalt no more be termed Forsaken; neither shall thy land any more be termed Desolate: but thou shalt be called Hephzibah, and thy land **Beulah**: for Yahuah delighteth in thee, and thy land shall be married.*

לֹא־יֵאָמֵר֩ לָ֨ךְ ע֜וֹד עֲזוּבָ֗ה וּלְאַרְצֵךְ֙
לֹא־יֵאָמֵ֥ר עוֹד֙ שְׁמָמָ֔ה כִּ֣י לָ֗ךְ יִקָּרֵא֙
חֶפְצִי־בָ֔הּ וּלְאַרְצֵ֖ךְ **בְּעוּלָ֑ה** כִּי־חָפֵ֤ץ
יְהוָה֙ בָּ֔ךְ וְאַרְצֵ֖ךְ תִּבָּעֵֽל

Isaiah 62:4

רעה (R-AH) Strong's #7453,7464,7468/ AHLB #1453

Tend

Satisfy needs

Lead to pasture

Being concerned

Thinking about

Seeking spiritual sustenance

Friend

Unified nation

Shepherd

Purpose

Aim

Desire

Man watches

Female companion

*Thou knowest my downsitting and mine upris-*
*ing, thou understandest **my thought** afar off.*

אַתָּה יָדַעְתָּ שִׁבְתִּי וְקוּמִי בַּנְתָּה
**לְרֵעִי** מֵרָחוֹק

Psalm 139:2

<u>חתן</u> (HhTN) Strong's #2859,2860-1/ AHLB #2224

Relate

Tie together for mutual satisfaction

Delightful relations

Wedding

Son in law

Infant at circumcision

Circumciser

To take hold of

A daughter's husband

Bridegroom

 Mother in law


*Neither shalt thou make marriages with them; thy*
*daughter thou shalt not give unto his son, nor his*
*daughter shalt thou take unto thy son.*

ו וְלֹא תִתְחַתֵּן בָּם בִּתְּךָ לֹא־תִתֵּן
לִבְנוֹ וּבִתּוֹ לֹא־תִקַּח לִבְנֶךָ

Deuteronomy 7:3

# Menstruation: Niddah (נדה)

## Classification of menstrual cycle phases

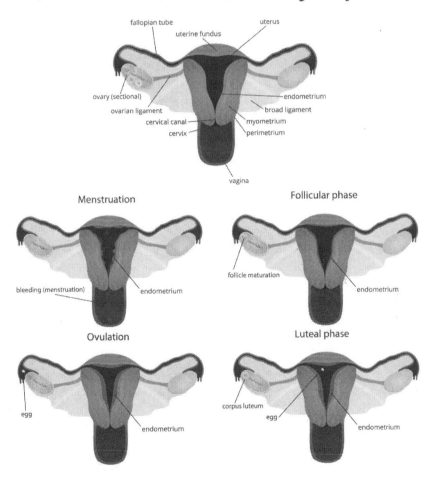

## ﹗ﻆﺩﻝ

נדה (NDH) Strong's #5079,5206/ AHLB #1303

Removal

Toss out

Cloth

Cut away

Distance due to impurity

Separation

*And if a woman have an issue, and her issue in her flesh be blood, she shall be **put apart** seven days: and whosoever toucheth her shall be unclean until the even.*

וְאִשָּׁה כִּי־תִהְיֶה זָבָה דָּם יִהְיֶה זֹבָהּ בִּבְשָׂרָהּ שִׁבְעַת יָמִים תִּהְיֶה **בְנִדָּתָהּ** וְכָל־

הַנֹּגֵעַ בָּהּ יִטְמָא עַד־הָעָרֶב

Leviticus 15:19

---

# Uncleanliness: Tame (טמא)

**טמא** (ThM) Strong's #2930/ AHLB #1197

Consummate

Lose purity

Defile

Lose freedom

To shut

To bind to

*Regard not them that have familiar spirits, neither seek after wizards, to be **defiled** by them: I am Yahuah your Elohim.*

אַל־תִּפְנוּ אֶל־הָאֹבֹת֙ וְאֶל־הַיִּדְּעֹנִ֔ים
אַל־ תְּבַקְשׁ֖וּ **לְטָמְאָה** בָהֶ֑ם אֲנִ֖י
יְהוָ֥ה אֱלֹהֵיכֶֽם
Leviticus 19:31

עָרָה (AhRH) Strong's #6168,6196/ AHLB #1365

Bare

Absorb impressions

Empty

Uncovering

Exposing

Being naked

Make sensitive

Destoy a protected place

*And if a man shall lie with a woman having her sickness, and shall uncover her nakedness; he* **_hath discovered_** *her fountain, and she hath uncovered the fountain of her blood: and both of them shall be cut off from among their people.*

וְאִישׁ אֲשֶׁר־יִשְׁכַּב אֶת־אִשָּׁה דָּוָה
וְגִלָּה אֶת־עֶרְוָתָהּ אֶת־מְקֹרָהּ
**הֶעֱרָה** וְהִיא גִּלְּתָה אֶת־מְקוֹר
דָּמֶיהָ וְנִכְרְתוּ שְׁנֵיהֶם מִקֶּרֶב עַמָּם

Leviticus 20:18

# Marriage: Eden (עדן)

עדן (EDN) Strong's #5727,5730/ AHLB #2528

Satisfy all needs

Delight

Give joy

Expensive shackles

Fancy food

Pleasure

Delicate

Luxurious

Therefore Sarah laughed within herself, saying, After I am waxed old shall I **have pleasure**, my lord being old also?

וַתִּצְחַק שָׂרָה בְּקִרְבָּהּ לֵאמֹר
אַחֲרֵי בְלֹתִי הָיְתָה־לִּי **עֶדְנָה**
וַאדֹנִי זָקֵן

Genesis 18:12

עטר <u>(ATR) Strong's #5849,5850/ AHLB #2538</u>

Delicate

Breast

Sustain

Being wrapped up in

To become the authority over

Go forth, O ye daughters of Zion, and behold king Solomon with the **crown** wherewith his mother crowned him in the day of his espousals, and in the day of the gladness of his heart.

צְאֶינָה ׀ וּרְאֶינָה בְּנָוֹת צִיֶּוֹן בַּמֶּלֶךְ
שְׁלֹמֹה **בָּעֲטָרָה** שֶׁעִטְּרָה־לָּוֹ אִמּוֹ
בְּיָוֹם חֲתֻנָּתֹו וּבְיָוֹם שִׂמְחַת לִבּוֹ

Song of Solomon 3:11

---

# Obey: Shama (שמע)

*O earth, earth, earth, hear the word of the LORD.*
**Jeremiah 22:29**

# ⊙ᴍʟʟ

שמע (ShMA) Strong's #5561,8033-4,8035-6/ AHLB #1473

Listening

Obey

Responding and doing

Action evoked by authority

Reciprocity because of position and worth

Now therefore **hearken**, O Israel, unto the statutes and unto the judgments, which I teach you, for to do *them*, that ye may live, and go in and possess the land which Yahuah Elohim of your fathers giveth you.

וְעַתָּה יִשְׂרָאֵל **שְׁמַע** אֶל־הַחֻקִּים֮

וְאֶל־הַמִּשְׁפָּטִים אֲשֶׁר אָנֹכִי מְלַמֵּד
אֶתְכֶם לַעֲשׂוֹת לְמַעַן תִּחְיוּ וּבָאתֶם
וִירִשְׁתֶּם
אֶת־הָאָרֶץ אֲשֶׁר יְהוָה אֱלֹהֵי אֲבֹתֵיכֶם
נֹתֵן לָכֶם

Deuteronomy 4:1

# ᛗᛚᛞ

שֵׁם <u>(ShM) Strong's #8034/ AHLB #1473</u>
Character or fame of a person
Name
What makes one worthy
Sweet aroma that is carried
Breath

O give thanks unto Yahuah; call upon **his name**:
make known his deeds among the people.

הוֹדוּ לַיהוָה קִרְאוּ **בִשְׁמוֹ** הוֹדִיעוּ
בָעַמִּים עֲלִילוֹתָיו

Psalm 105:1

שעה (ShAH) Strong's #8159,8160/ AHLB #1476

Delight
 Caring for with delight
Looking out for danger
Destroy the enemy
Object of constant care
Turning in acceptance

___I will delight myself___ in thy statutes: I will not forget thy word.

בְּחֻקֹּתֶיךָ **אֶשְׁתַּעֲשָׁע** לֹא אֶשְׁכַּח
דְּבָרֶךָ
Psalm 119:16

STUDY FORTY-THREE

# Stronghold or Fortress: Tsud (צוד)

**צוד** (TsWD) Strong's #6718/ AHLB #1395

Lie down to sleep

Ambush

Fortress

Save for

Vulnerable side

Trap

Catch

Hunt

Game

Provision

**Positive:**

I will say of Yahuah, *He is* my refuge and my fortress: my Elohim; in him will I trust.

אֹמַ֗ר לַֽ֭יהוָה מַחְסִ֣י וּמְצוּדָתִ֑י אֱלֹהַ֗י אֶבְטַח־בּֽוֹ

Psalm 91:2

**Negative:**

> My net also will I spread upon him, and he shall
> be taken in my snare: and I will bring him to
> Babylon *to* the land of the Chaldeans; yet shall
> he not see it, though he shall die there.

וּפָרַשְׂתִּי אֶת־רִשְׁתִּי עָלָיו וְנִתְפַּשׂ
בִּמְצוּדָתִי וְהֵבֵאתִי אֹתוֹ בָבֶלָה אֶרֶץ
כַּשְׂדִּים וְאוֹתָהּ לֹא־יִרְאֶה וְשָׁם יָמוּת

Ezekiel 12:13

ציד

**צִיד** (TsYD) Strong's #3684,3688,5528/ AHLB #2275

Meat

Hunt

Game

The product of the hunt

**Positive:**

> I will abundantly bless her provision: I will sat-
> isfy her poor with bread.

צֵידָהּ בָּרֵךְ אֲבָרֵךְ אֶבְיוֹנֶיהָ אַשְׂבִּיעַ
לָחֶם

Psalm 132:15

**Negative:**

He was a mighty hunter before Yahuah: wherefore it is said, Even as Nimrod the mighty
hunter before Yahuah.

הַ הוּא־הָיָה גִּבֹּר־צַיִד לִפְנֵי יְהוָה
עַל־כֵּן יֵאָמַר כְּנִמְרֹד גִּבּוֹר צַיִד
לִפְנֵי יְהוָה

Genesis 10:9

<u>פחה</u> (PKhH) Strong's #6341 AHLB #1376

Calamities

Plots

Traps

Rule

Govern

Put out fire

**Positive:**

The wicked have laid a snare for me: yet I erred
not from thy precepts.

נָתְנ֬וּ רְשָׁעִים פַּ֣ח לִ֑י וּ֝מִפִּקּוּדֶ֗יךָ לֹ֣א תָעִֽיתִי

Psalm 119:110

**Negative:**

Know for a certainty that Yahuah your Elohim will no more drive out *any of* these nations from before you; but they shall be snares and traps unto you, and scourges in your sides, and thorns in your eyes, until ye perish from off this good land which Yahuah your Elohim hath given you.

יָד֨וֹעַ תֵּדְע֜וּ כִּ֣י לֹ֤א יוֹסִיף֙ יְהֹוָ֣ה אֱלֹהֵיכֶ֔ם לְהוֹרִ֛ישׁ אֶת־הַגּוֹיִ֥ם הָאֵ֖לֶּה מִלִּפְנֵיכֶ֑ם וְהָי֨וּ לָכֶ֜ם לְפַ֣ח וּלְמוֹקֵ֗שׁ וּלְשֹׁטֵ֤ט בְּצִדֵּיכֶם֙ וְלִצְנִנִ֣ים בְּעֵינֵיכֶ֔ם עַד־אֲבָדְכֶ֗ם מֵעַ֨ל הָאֲדָמָ֤ה הַטּוֹבָה֙ הַזֹּ֔את אֲשֶׁר֙ נָתַ֣ן לָכֶ֔ם יְהֹוָ֖ה אֱלֹהֵיכֶֽם

Joshua 23:13

## צדה (TsDH) Strong's #6658/ AHLB #1395

Target

Directing Destruction

Lay down

Ambush

Destroy

**Positive:**

And if a man lie not in wait, but Elohim deliver *him* into his hand; then I will appoint thee a
place whither he shall flee.

$$\text{וַאֲשֶׁר֙ לֹ֣א צָדָ֔ה וְהָאֱלֹהִ֖ים אִנָּ֣ה}$$
$$\text{לְיָד֑וֹ וְשַׂמְתִּ֤י לְךָ֙ מָק֔וֹם אֲשֶׁ֥ר יָנ֖וּס}$$
$$\text{שָֽׁמָּה}$$

Exodus 21:13

**Negative:**

Moreover, my father, see, yea, see the skirt of
thy robe in my hand: for in that I cut off the skirt
of thy robe, and killed thee not, know thou and
see that *there is* neither evil nor transgression in
mine hand, and I have not sinned against thee;
yet thou huntest my soul to take it.

$$\text{וְאָבִ֣י רְאֵ֗ה גַּ֣ם רְאֵ֞ה אֶת־כְּנַ֤ף}$$
$$\text{מְעִֽילְךָ֙ בְּיָדִ֔י כִּ֤י בְּכָרְתִי֙ אֶת־כְּנַ֤ף}$$
$$\text{מְעִֽילְךָ֙ וְלֹ֣א הֲרַגְתִּ֔יךָ דַּ֣ע וּרְאֵ֗ה כִּ֠י}$$

אֵין בְּיָדִי רָעָה וָפֶּשַׁע
וְלֹא־חָטָאתִי לָךְ וְאַתָּה צֹדֶה אֶת־
נַפְשִׁי
לְקַחְתָּהּ

1 Samuel 24:11

<u>יצר</u> (YTsR) Strong's #3335/ AHLB #2028

Senseless

Brutish

Burn

Kindle fire

## Positive:

And Yahuah Elohim formed man of the dust of
the ground, and breathed into his nostrils the
breath of life; and man became a living soul.

וַיִּיצֶר יְהֹוָה אֱלֹהִים אֶת־הָאָדָם
עָפָר מִן־הָאֲדָמָה וַיִּפַּח בְּאַפָּיו
נִשְׁמַת חַיִּים וַיְהִי הָאָדָם לְנֶפֶשׁ
חַיָּה

Genesis 2:7

**Negative:**

Then Jacob was greatly afraid and dis-
tressed: and he divided the people
that *was* with him, and the flocks, and
herds, and the camels, into two bands;

וַיִּירָ֨א יַעֲקֹ֜ב מְאֹ֗ד וַיֵּ֣צֶר ל֑וֹ וַיַּ֜חַץ אֶת־
הָעָ֣ם אֲשֶׁר־אִתּ֗וֹ וְאֶת־הַצֹּ֛אן וְאֶת־
הַבָּקָ֥ר וְהַגְּמַלִּ֖ים לִשְׁנֵ֥י מַחֲנֽוֹת

Genesis 32:7

STUDY FORTY-FOUR

# Sex: Yada (ידע)

לּדּ⊙

**ידע** (YDA) Strong's #3045/ AHLB #1085

Knowing the difference between
Bringing to senses
Awakening
The door of the body is the eye
Window to the soul
Intimate relationship

And Adam **knew** Eve his wife; and she conceived, and bare Cain, and said, I have gotten a
man from Yahuah.

וְהָ֣אָדָ֔ם **יָדַ֖ע** אֶת־חַוָּ֣ה אִשְׁתּ֑וֹ וַתַּ֙הַר֙
וַתֵּ֣לֶד אֶת־קַ֔יִן וַתֹּ֕אמֶר קָנִ֥יתִי אִ֖ישׁ
אֶת־יְהוָֽה

Genesis 4:1

**בוא** (BWA) Strong's #935,3997/ AHLB #1024

To fill a void

Empty space

To fill a space by entering

Fulfill a desire

To increase produce

A place of entering

A gate or passage

And it came to pass in the evening, that he took Leah his daughter, and brought her to him; and he went in unto her.

וַיְהִי בָעֶרֶב וַיִּקַּח אֶת־לֵאָה בִתּוֹ
וַיָּבֵא אֹתָהּ אֵלָיו **וַיָּבֹא** אֵלֶיהָ

Genesis 29:23

# שׁגה

**שגה** (ShGH) Strong's #7686/ AHLB #1463

Be ravished

To go astray

Double burden

Do it again

Err
*Let her be as the loving hind and pleasant roe;
let her breasts satisfy thee at all times; and be
thou **ravished** always with her love.*

אַיֶּלֶת אֲהָבִים וְיַעֲלַת־חֵן דַּדֶּיהָ
יְרַוֻּךָ בְכָל־עֵת בְּאַהֲבָתָהּ **תִשְׁגֶּה**
תָמִיד

Proverbs 5:19

# ששם

<u>שכב</u> (ShKhB) Strong's #7901-3/ AHLB #2834
Lay down to copulate
Sex
To lay captive

And if a man **entice** a maid that is not betrothed,
and lie with her, he shall surely endow her to be
his wife

וְכִי־**יְפַתֶּה** אִישׁ בְּתוּלָה אֲשֶׁר לֹא־
אֹרָשָׂה וְשָׁכַב עִמָּהּ מָהֹר יִמְהָרֶנָּה
לֹו לְאִשָּׁה

Exodus 22:16

# Covenant: Nakar (נכר)

נכר (NKhR) Strong's #5234/ AHLB #2406

Isolate

Recognize individually

Respect

Discern

Pay attention to

Acknowledge

Care for someone or something

To know something you didn't know before

*And her mother in law said unto her, Where hast thou gleaned to day? and where wroughtest thou? blessed be **he that did take knowledge** of thee. And she shewed her mother in law with whom she had wrought, and said, The man's name with whom I wrought to day is Boaz.*

וַתֹּאמֶר לָהּ חֲמוֹתָהּ אֵיפֹה לִקַּטְתְּ
הַיּוֹם וְאָנָה עָשִׂית יְהִי **מַכִּירֵךְ** בָּרוּךְ
וַתַּגֵּד לַחֲמוֹתָהּ אֵת אֲשֶׁר־עָשְׂתָה
עִמּוֹ וַתֹּאמֶר שֵׁם הָאִישׁ אֲשֶׁר
עָשִׂיתִי עִמּוֹ הַיּוֹם בֹּעַז

Ruth 2:19

# ⊼⊡†

**ברת** (BRT) Strong's #1267,1285/ AHLB #1043

Rejuvenate

Eat a meal

Feeding

Separate out parts

Choicest

Confederacy

*And he was there with Yahuah forty days and
forty nights; he did neither eat bread, nor drink
water. And he wrote upon the tables the words
of the* **covenant***, the ten commandments.*

וַיְהִי־שָׁם עִם־יְהֹוָה אַרְבָּעִים יוֹם
וְאַרְבָּעִים לַיְלָה לֶחֶם לֹא אָכַל

וּמַיִם לֹא שָׁתָה וַיִּכְתֹּב עַל־הַלֻּחֹת
אֵת דִּבְרֵי **הַבְּרִית** עֲשֶׂרֶת הַדְּבָרִים

Exodus 34:28

שׁרת

<u>כרת</u> (KhRT) Strong's #3772/ AHLB #2291

Cut off
Separating
Cutting an animal to join

*And they said, We saw certainly that the LORD
was with thee: and we said, Let there be now an
oath betwixt us, even betwixt us and thee, **and
let us make** a covenant with thee;*

וַיֹּאמְרוּ רָאוֹ רָאִינוּ כִּי־הָיָה יְהוָה
עִמָּךְ וַנֹּאמֶר תְּהִי נָא אָלָה בֵּינוֹתֵינוּ
בֵּינֵינוּ וּבֵינֶךָ **וְנִכְרְתָה** בְרִית עִמָּךְ

Genesis 26:28

<u>ידע</u> (YDA) Strong's #3045/ AHLB #1085

Knowing the difference between

Bringing to senses
Awakening
The door of the body is the eye
Window to the soul
Intimate relationship

*And Adam **knew** Eve his wife; and she con-*
*ceived, and bare Cain, and said, I have gotten a*
*man from the LORD.*

וְהָ֣אָדָ֔ם **יָדַ֖ע** אֶת־חַוָּ֣ה אִשְׁתּ֑וֹ
וַתַּ֙הַר֙ וַתֵּ֣לֶד אֶת־קַ֔יִן וַתֹּ֕אמֶר
קָנִ֥יתִי אִ֖ישׁ אֶת־יְהוָֽה

Genesis 4:1

## STUDY FORTY-SIX

# Divorce: Karath (כרת)

*Yahusha answered, "It was because of your hardness of heart that Moses permitted you to divorce your wives; but it was not this way from the beginning.*
**Matthew 19:8**

# †𐤀ש‎

כרת (KhRT) Strong's #3748,3772/ AHLB #2291

Cut off

Separating

Cutting the covenant

Cut short

Cutting off from the family tree

Cut off from the husband

And I will give the men that have transgressed my covenant, which have not performed the words of the covenant which they had made before me, when they **cut** the calf in twain, and passed between the parts thereof,

וְנָתַתִּי אֶת־הָאֲנָשִׁים הָעֹבְרִים֙ אֶת־
בְּרִתִי אֲשֶׁר לֹא־הֵקִימוּ֙ אֶת־דִּבְרֵ֣י
הַבְּרִית אֲשֶׁר **כָּרְתוּ** לְפָנָ֑י הָעֵ֕גֶל
אֲשֶׁר **כָּרְתוּ** לִשְׁנַ֔יִם וַיַּעַבְר֖וּ בֵּ֥ין
בְּתָרָיו

Jeremiah 34:18

# ▣▣⊔/ш▣

<u>שלח</u> (ShLKh) Strong's #7971-3/ AHLB #2842

Send

Move to a goal

Abandoning of people

Allowing something to move

Move in balanced way

For Yahuah, the Elohim of Israel, saith that he hateth **putting away**: for one covereth violence with his garment, saith Yahuah of hosts: therefore take heed to your spirit, that ye deal not treacherously.

כִּי־שָׂנֵ֣א שַׁלַּ֗ח אָמַ֞ר יְהוָ֤ה אֱלֹהֵ֣י
יִשְׂרָאֵ֔ל וְכִסָּ֤ה חָמָס֙ עַל־לְבוּשׁ֔וֹ
אָמַ֖ר יְהוָ֣ה צְבָא֑וֹת וְנִשְׁמַרְתֶּ֖ם

בְּרוּחֲכֶם וְלֹא תִבְגֹּדוּ

Malachi 2:16

## 𐤔𐤀𐤁

גרש (GRSh) Strong's #1645-6AHLB #2089

Send out to pasture

Eviction

Expel

 Put out

Divorce

Put outside the city

Dismiss

*They shall not take a wife that is a whore, or pro-fane; neither shall they take a woman* **put away** *from her husband: for he is holy unto his Elohim.*

אִשָּׁה זֹנָה וַחֲלָלָה לֹא יִקָּחוּ וְאִשָּׁה **גְרוּשָׁה** מֵאִישָׁהּ לֹא יִקָּחוּ כִּי־קָדֹשׁ הוּא לֵאלֹהָיו

Leviticus 21:7

---

# Adultery/Fornication: Zanah (זנה)

## נאף (NAPh) Strong's #5003-4/ AHLB #2406

Heated passion

Heavy breathing

Flared Nostrils

Break wedlock

Commit adultery

Turn from one to another

*And the man that committeth **adultery** with another man's wife, even he that committeth adultery with his neighbour's wife, the adulterer and the adulteress shall surely be put to death.*

וְאִישׁ אֲשֶׁר **יִנְאַף** אֶת־אֵשֶׁת אִישׁ אֲשֶׁר יִנְאַף אֶת־אֵשֶׁת רֵעֵהוּ מוֹת־יוּמַת הַנֹּאֵף וְהַנֹּאָפֶת

Leviticus 20:10

זָנָה (ZNH) Strong's #2181,2183-4,8457/ AHLB #1152

Whoredom

Defect

Be unfaithful

Straying

Prostituting

Forsake

Harlot

To be spread around

Literally a mattock or a hoe

A tool for cutting or tearing something apart

*Lest thou make a covenant with the inhabitants of the land, and they go a **whoring** after their Elohims, and do sacrifice unto their Elohims, and one call thee, and thou eat of his sacrifice;.*

פֶּן־תִּכְרֹת בְּרִית לְיוֹשֵׁב הָאָרֶץ

**וְזָנוּ** ׀ אַחֲרֵי אֱלֹהֵיהֶם וְזָבְחוּ

לֵאלֹהֵיהֶם וְקָרָא לְךָ וְאָכַלְתָּ

מִזִּבְחוֹ

Exodus 34:15

# ⊥⊔⊓‑⊖‑

קדשׁ (QDSh) Strong's #6942,6948/ AHLB #2700

Whore
Set apart for special function
Separating and joining to something
Reserving and prohibiting from further use
Making independent
Being immoral

*Then he asked the men of that place, saying, Where is the harlot, that was openly by the way side? And they said, There was no* **harlot** *in this place.*

וַיִּשְׁאַל אֶת־אַנְשֵׁי מְקֹמָהּ לֵאמֹר
אַיֵּה הַקְּדֵשָׁה הִוא בָעֵינַיִם עַל־
הַדָּרֶךְ וַיֹּאמְרוּ לֹא־הָיְתָה בָזֶה
**קדשׁה**

Genesis 38:21

STUDY FORTY-EIGHT

# Covering: Kasah (כסה)

כסה/א (CSH) Strong's #3678,3677/ AHLB #1245

Throne

Seat of Authority

Cover

Conceal a person

Withdraw from sight

Elevated seat

Armor (Scales)

A mark or sign upon a person as protection

Amulet

Separate

Designated time

Allocate

*Thou shalt be over my house, and according unto thy word shall all my people be ruled: only in the throne will I be greater than thou.*

אַתָּה תִּהְיֶה עַל־בֵּיתִי וְעַל־פִּיךָ
יִשַּׁק כָּל־עַמִּי רַק הַכִּסֵּא אֶגְדַּל מִמֶּךָּ

Genesis 41:40

לאט <u></u> (LAT) Strong's #3813/ AHLB #1262

Cover

Veil

Secret

Hide the face of woman

Enchant secretly

Authority contained

Camouflaging

Wrap.

But the king **covered** his face, and the king cried with a loud voice, O my son Absalom, O Absalom, my son, my son!

וְהַמֶּ֫לֶךְ **לָאַט** אֶת־פָּנָיו וַיִּזְעַק
הַמֶּ֫לֶךְ קוֹל גָּדוֹל בְּנִי אַבְשָׁלוֹם
אַבְשָׁלוֹם בְּנִי בְנִי

2 Samuel 19:4

<u>כפר</u> (CPhR) Strong's #3722/ AHLB #2283

Protect or correct wrong

Reconcile

Forgiveness

Purge

Appease

Pardon

Cover

Atonement

Covering for a debt

Iniquities prevail against me: *as for* our transgressions, thou **shalt purge them away**.

דִּבְרֵי עֲוֹנֹת גָּבְרוּ מֶנִּי פְּשָׁעֵינוּ אַתָּה
**תְּכַפְּרֵם**

Psalm 65:3

<u>ס/שלם</u> (SLM) Strong's #8008/ AHLB #2483

Garment (covering)

Restitution

Thy lips, O *my* spouse, drop *as* the honeycomb: honey and milk *are* under thy tongue; and the

smell of thy **garments** _is_ like the smell of Leba-
non.

נֹפֶת תִּטֹּפְנָה שִׂפְתוֹתַיִךְ כַּלָּה
דְּבַשׁ וְחָלָב תַּחַת לְשׁוֹנֵךְ וְרֵיחַ
**שַׂלְמֹתַיִךְ** כְּרֵיחַ לְבָנוֹן

Song of Solomon 4:11

STUDY FORTY-NINE

# Work: Abad (עבד)

עבד (ABD) Strong's #5647-52/ AHLB #2518

Profession
Bondage/ Being a slave
Perform out of obligation
Requirement
Temple service
Provide service
Subject to another's will
Directing energies to another's goal
Constrain by external force
Servant

*Go therefore now, and* **work***; for there shall no straw be given you, yet shall ye deliver the tale of bricks.*

וְעַתָּה לְכוּ **עִבְדוּ** וְתֶבֶן לֹא־יִנָּתֵן לָכֶם
וְתֹכֶן לְבֵנִים תִּתֵּנוּ

Exodus 5:18

# ⟨symbols⟩

יָגַע (YGA) Strong's #3021/ AHLB #1062

Work that brings about heavy breathing and weariness
Gasp for air
Tire
Exert oneself

**Labour** not to be rich: cease from thine own wisdom.

אַל־**תִּיגַע** לְהַעֲשִׁיר מִבִּינָתְךָ חֲדָל

Proverbs 23:4

# ⟨symbols⟩

עש/סה (ASH) Strong's #6213/ AHLB #1360

Doing something that causes increase
Make
Create
Forming
Causing to grow

*But the seventh day is the sabbath of Yahuah thy Elohim: in it thou shalt not do any* **work**, *thou, nor thy son, nor thy daughter, nor thy manservant, nor thy maidservant, nor thine ox, nor thine ass,* *nor any of thy cattle, nor thy stranger that is within thy gates; that thy manservant and thy maidservant may rest as well as thou. And remember that thou wast a servant in the land of Egypt, and that Yahuah thy Elohim brought thee out thence through a mighty hand and by a stretched out arm: therefore Yahuah thy Elohim commanded thee to keep the sabbath day.*

וְיוֹם֙ הַשְּׁבִיעִ֔י שַׁבָּ֖ת ׀ לַיהוָ֣ה אֱלֹהֶ֑יךָ
לֹ֣א **תַעֲשֶׂ֣ה** כָל־מְלָאכָ֡ה אַתָּ֣ה וּבִנְךָֽ־
וּבִתֶּ֣ךָ וְעַבְדְּךָֽ־וַאֲמָתֶ֡ךָ וְשֽׁוֹרְךָ֩ וַחֲמֹֽרְךָ֨
וְכָל־בְּהֶמְתֶּ֜ךָ וְגֵֽרְךָ֣ אֲשֶׁ֣ר בִּשְׁעָרֶ֗יךָ
לְמַ֗עַן
יָנ֛וּחַ עַבְדְּךָ֥ וַאֲמָתְךָ֖ כָּמ֑וֹךָ וְזָכַרְתָּ֗ כִּֽ֣י
יְ־עֶ֣בֶד הָיִ֣יתָ ׀ בְּאֶ֣רֶץ מִצְרַ֗יִם וַיֹּצִֽאֲךָ֩
יְהוָ֨ה אֱלֹהֶ֤יךָ מִשָּׁם֙ בְּיָ֤ד חֲזָקָ֔ה
וּבִזְרֹ֖עַ נְטוּיָ֑ה עַל־כֵּ֗ן צִוְּךָ֙ יְהוָ֣ה
אֱלֹהֶ֔יךָ לַעֲשׂ֖וֹת אֶת־יֹ֥ום הַשַּׁבָּֽת
Deuteronomy 5:14-15

# 𝑙ᴺᵁᵂ/ 𝑙ᴬᵁᵂ

לך/לאך (LAKh) Strong's #4399/ AHLB #1264

Walk

Message

Defend Against

Serve

Work which completes a goal

*Six days shall work be done: but the seventh day is the sabbath of rest, an holy convocation; ye shall do no work therein: it is the sabbath of Yahuah in all your dwellings.*

ו שֵׁ֣שֶׁת יָמִים֮ תֵּעָשֶׂ֣ה **מְלָאכָה֒**
וּבַיּ֣וֹם הַשְּׁבִיעִ֗י שַׁבַּ֤ת שַׁבָּתוֹן֙ מִקְרָא־
קֹ֔דֶשׁ כָּל־מְלָאכָ֖ה לֹ֣א תַעֲשׂ֑וּ שַׁבָּ֥ת
הוא֙ לַֽיהֹוָ֔ה בְּכֹ֖ל מֽוֹשְׁבֹתֵיכֶֽם

Leviticus 23:3

# 𝑙𝑙◉/𝑙◉

על/עלל (ELL) Strong's #5953/ AHLB #1357

Abuse

Work

Yoke

Experience the staff
Fruit developing
Working over another
Work performed without consideration
Leading to a goal
Developing child

*And that thou mayest tell in the ears of thy son,
and of thy son's son, what things I have **wrought**
in Egypt, and my signs which I have done among
them; that ye may know how that I am Yahuah.*

וּלְמַ֡עַן תְּסַפֵּר֩ בְּאָזְנֵ֨י בִנְךָ֜ וּבֶן־בִּנְךָ֗
אֵ֣ת אֲשֶׁ֤ר הִתְעַלַּ֙לְתִּי֙ בְּמִצְרַ֔יִם וְאֶת־
אֹתֹתַ֖י אֲשֶׁר־שַׂ֣מְתִּי בָ֑ם וִֽידַעְתֶּ֖ם כִּֽי־
אֲנִ֥י יְהוָֽה
Exodus 10:2

פעל (PAL) Strong's #6466-8/ AHLB #2622
Work hard to a goal
Laboring
Creating
Deeds
Do
Perform

*Give them according to their deeds, and according to the wickedness of their endeavours: give them after the work of their hands; render to them their desert.*

יְשַׁלֵּ֤ם יְהוָה֙ פָּעֳלֵ֔ךְ וּתְהִ֤י
מַשְׂכֻּרְתֵּךְ֙ שְׁלֵמָ֔ה מֵעִ֖ם יְהוָ֣ה אֱלֹהֵ֣י
יִשְׂרָאֵ֑ל אֲשֶׁר־בָּ֖את לַחֲס֥וֹת תַּֽחַת־
כְּנָפָֽיו

Ruth 2:12

<u>יצר</u> (YTsR) Strong's #3335, 3336/ AHLB #1411

A pressing

A burden

Forming something

Pressing thought

Purpose

Intent

Planning

*The smith with the tongs both worketh in the coals, and **fashioneth** it with hammers, and worketh it with the strength of his arms: yea, he is hungry, and his strength faileth: he drinketh no water, and is faint.*

חָרַשׁ בַּרְזֶל מַעֲצָד וּפָעַל בַּפֶּחָם
וּבַמַּקָּבוֹת **יִצְּרֵהוּ** וַיִּפְעָלֵהוּ בִּזְרוֹעַ
כֹּחוֹ גַּם־רָעֵב וְאֵין כֹּחַ לֹא־שָׁתָה
מַיִם וַיִּיעָף

Isaiah 44:12

פלא (PLA) Strong's #6381-2/ AHLB #1380

A great action

Wonderous act

Freely vowing

Diverge from the norm

Separate


*Sing unto him, sing psalms unto him: talk ye of*
*all his **wondrous works**.*

שִׁירוּ־לוֹ זַמְּרוּ־לוֹ יחוּ בְּכָל־
נִפְלְאוֹתָיו

Psalm 105:2

---

# Rest: Shabbat (שבת)

# †ﬦɰ

**שבת** (ShBTh) Strong's #7676 AHLB #2812

Day set aside for resting or celebration

Ceasing of work

7ᵗʰ day (Only day with a name)

Cease on going activity

Yah's day of rest

Cease

*And he said unto them, This is that which Yahuah hath said, To morrow is the rest of the holy **sabbath** unto Yahuah: bake that which ye will bake to day, and seethe that ye will seethe; and that which remaineth over lay up for you to be kept until the morning.*

וַיֹּאמֶר אֲלֵהֶם הוּא אֲשֶׁר דִּבֶּר יְהוָֹה שַׁבָּתוֹן **שַׁבַּת**־קֹדֶשׁ לַיהוָה מָחָר אֵת אֲשֶׁר־תֹּאפוּ אֵפוּ וְאֵת אֲשֶׁר־תְּבַשְּׁלוּ

בַּשֵּׁלוּ וְאֵת כָּל־הָעֹדֵף הַנִּיחוּ לָכֶם
לְמִשְׁמֶרֶת עַד־הַבֹּקֶר

Exodus 16:23

חדל **חדל** (HhDL) Strong's #2308,2310/ AHLB #2148
Refrain from continuing an action
Refuse
Rejected
End

*So the LORD scattered them abroad from thence upon the face of all the earth: and they **left off** to build the city.*

וַיָּפֶץ יְהֹוָה אֹתָם מִשָּׁם עַל־פְּנֵי
כָל־הָאָרֶץ **וַיַּחְדְּלוּ** לִבְנֹת הָעִיר

Genesis 11:8

השב **השב** (HShV) Strong's #2803-4,4284/ AHLB #2213
Resigning from plans
Joining

Thinking
Turning over thoughts
Design or purpose
Combining thoughts
Working
Skillfully

*But as for you, ye thought evil against me; but Elohim meant it unto good, to bring to pass, as it is this day, to save much people alive.*

וְאַתֶּם חֲשַׁבְתֶּם עָלַי רָעָה אֱלֹהִים
חֲשָׁבָהּ לְטֹבָה לְמַעַן עֲשֹׂה כַּיּוֹם
הַזֶּה לְהַחֲיֹת עַם־
רָב

Genesis 50:20

## Special Thank You:

*Amarayahu & Emunah*
You are truly a Yah send. Thank you for showing me when my "hands" are building and even more importantly when they are destroying. It doesn't take a rocket scientist to spot foolishness, but it takes family to stand next to you with a hammer and nail to rebuild what has been destroyed.

*To my "Girls":*
I put that in parentheses because I dare not take away from the reverence and honor that your true position holds. Mom and Aunt Monae… I lack words for what it means to have family in this walk and even more so what it means to be privileged to have you as sisters in the faith. You two are the reason that I can do all that I do and also the ones who are my counselors and prayer warriors when I don't know how to move. You challenge me to walk circumspect to the father as well as to be kind and humble in the face of adversity. I love you with all my heart!

*Moreh Yoshiyahu Dauid*
My teacher, My friend, and in this my muse. We had a rough year lol! Yah has shown us how to walk together and how to agree. He has fused our purposes, but even greater he has solidified His reason for there being an "US". I thank you for remaining steadfast. I thank you for listening to all the lessons that came to my head for each chapter that have yet to be taught, and even more for standing on the truth at all times. You are it!

# ABOUT THE AUTHOR

Huldah is of Malagasy Hebrew descendant. It is the oral tradition of her family that they were taken from Madagascar on a Dutch slave ship to Holland. It was from Holland that her family made it to North Carolina. Huldah is a college graduate and an Educator. She currently lives in California. She is Married to the love of her life, and they have two beautiful daughters. Her passion and focus is the liberation of women and children through truth of their rich cultural heritage.

# Notes

# Notes

# Notes

67163051R00128

Made in the USA
Middletown, DE
19 March 2018